TALK IS CHEAP

The Americas Group
9200 Sunset Blvd., Suite 404
Los Angeles, California 90069
USA

ISBN:
0-935047-12-3
Library of Congress Catalog Card Number:
91-071599

Library of Congress Cataloging-in-Publication Data

Harris, Godfrey, 1937-
    Talk is cheap : promoting your business through word of mouth advertising / Godfrey Harris with Gregrey J Harris. -- 1st ed.
    136p. cm.
    Includes bibliographical references and index.
    ISBN 0-935047-12-3 (softbound) : $9.95
    1. Customer relations. 2. Customer service--Public opinion.
3. Consumer satisfaction. 4. Advertising. 5. Oral communication.
I. Harris, Gregrey J., 1962-   . II. Title.
HF5415.5.H29 1991
658.8'12--dc20
                                                        91-604
                                                        CIP

Printed in the United States of America
Delta Lithograph Co.

TALK IS CHEAP

Promoting
Your
Business
Through
Word
of
Mouth
Advertising

Godfrey Harris
with
Gregrey J Harris

ALSO BY GODFREY HARRIS

The Fascination of Ivory
Invasion (with David S. Behar)
The Ultimate Black Book
The Panamanian Perspective
Promoting International Tourism (with Kenneth M. Katz)
Commercial Translations (with Charles Sonabend)
From Trash to Treasure (with Barbara DeKovner-Mayer)
Panama's Position
The Quest for Foreign Affairs Officers (with Francis Fielder)
The History of Sandy Hook, New Jersey
Outline of Social Sciences
Outline of Western Civilization

TABLE OF CONTENTS

A CONVERSATION
OVERHEARD AT THE OFFICE

JOE   *Do either of you know where I can take my film for developing? My parents are anxious to see the pictures from their anniversary party last week.*

TOM   *Well, stay clear of Discount Photo in the lobby. I've had nothing but trouble with them.*

JOE   *What trouble? You give them the film and they put it through a machine and you get the photos back, right?*

TOM   *Yeah, right. The pictures look fine, the price is OK, but they never seem to be able to deliver within the hour they promise. Every time I've dropped film off on the way to lunch and asked to pick the pictures up on the way back to the office, they say "no problem." But they always do have a problem. They never keep their promise and, worse, they don't seem to care.*

SUE   *I take our film over to The Clever Camera on Maple.*

JOE   *Are their prices that good?*

SUE   *Not especially. In fact, the drug store probably beats them with all of the special promotions and coupons they have.*

TOM   *So why do you recommend them?*

SUE   *It's the little things, I guess. Their quality is about the same as everyone else's and they aren't super fast. I just like taking my business there. Gary, the owner, always greets me by name even though I'm only in there once a month or so. When I had a problem getting an old battery out, he worked on it and never charged me. When I wanted to buy my nephew a camera, he was really knowledgeable about the best choices. But I guess the real reason I like going there is that Gary is always doing something new to make his customers feel special.*

JOE   *Good enough for me. Let's go over there. Sounds like he's someone Tom and I should get to know, too.*

BACKGROUND

For too long now, word of mouth promotion has been appreciated, but unmanaged—generally understood as a factor in the success of any business, but left alone to develop of its own volition. While personally employed as a tool by some enterprising owners, word of mouth advertising has seldom been shaped so that *customers* can generate comments on behalf of a business.

But there is no doubt that you can develop effective ways to stimulate and sustain positive discussions about your products, services, or activities, while avoiding negative comments before they do damage.

> *In short, positive word of mouth comments need not be left to luck, and negative commentary need never be left to fester.*

While word of mouth promotion sounds as if it may be connected to traditional *advertising* or related to *public relations,* it is actually a different type of **commercial communication.**

> **Word of mouth promotion is what people verbalize to others about specific products, services, or activities.**

This means that word of mouth promotion should not be confused with paid testimonial comments by celebrities, printed promotional blurbs by critics, or the broad reputation achieved by organizations over time. It is, in brief, an individual person-to-person undertaking.^

---

^ The carat mark indicates that a comment related to an aspect of the text can be found under the appropriate page number in the Bibliographical Notes section beginning at p. 125.

To keep the distinction among *advertising*, *public relations*, and *word of mouth promotion* clearly in mind, note the following comparison:

- If a concert promoter **buys** newspaper space to urge other businesses to help sponsor a free concert, that's *advertising*.

- If other businesses learn about the possibility of helping to sponsor a free concert through a newspaper **article**, that's *public relations*.

- But if one CEO **tells** another CEO about the advantages of becoming one of the sponsors of a free concert, that's *word of mouth!*

The three forms of commercial communication can reinforce each other. For example, public relations gives advertising credibility; advertising, in turn, provides public relations with greater receptivity. And both, individually or in tandem, can be the impetus for stimulating word of mouth discussions. Chemical Bank recently recognized the relationship in an advertisement in *The New York Times Magazine*. The headline reads: "Most of our clients are referred by a source far more compelling than any advertising." Underneath Chemical Bank noted: "...our clients themselves are our single most reliable" means of acquiring new accounts.

Even those business people who have clearly recognized the value of word of mouth discussions are not entirely sure how best to *encourage* more of them.

- In the **entertainment business**, for instance, what people say and how they say it has become crucial to the staying power of a film or play. As a result, these comments are often replicated for   insertion into paid media advertising. For example, Disney's Touchstone Films is reported to have spent some $10 million in 1990 on ads featuring movie-goers telling TV viewers that *Pretty Woman* was a film not to be missed.^

- Among **food companies**, traditional advertising is often used to *introduce* new products, but consumer conversations about those products determines whether they will *remain* on supermarket shelves. One study estimates that homemakers rank word of mouth as the "single most important influence on a decision to try a food product." Campbell Soup, for one, reports that 90 percent of the time, people purchase a new soup when someone has personally recommended it..*

- In **medical and legal practices** as well as most other **professional firms**, referrals still bring in the bulk of new patients and clients, but most doctors and lawyers can only *hope* that their successful results get discussed. As an example of the importance of word of mouth advertising to service businesses, one survey of **security companies** indicates that 30 percent are chosen because of word of mouth recommendations.*

- Among **illegal and socially marginal enterprises**—prostitution, drug dealing, black market trading, spouse swapping—word of mouth commentary may be the *only* form of promotion available, but dangerous to encourage.

Despite the random appearance of word of mouth promotion, it can be the **most effective** *and* **least expensive** form of promotion. That, in fact, is the good news. The bad news is that the line between what will stimulate *positive* word of mouth comments or cause *negative* ones is a very thin one. And in an age that loves gossip, negative word of mouth comments seem to spread faster than positive ones.^

A tourism consultant in England sees the problem another way. He calculates that 70 percent of theme park business arises from positive word of mouth comments while 80 percent of the problems of the industry can be traced to negative comments.* Look at the positive/ negative word of mouth comparison in the following observations by the authors:

---

* The asterisk denotes that a source for a quotation or statistic can be found under the appropriate page number in the Bibliographical Notes section beginning at p. 125.

At the **Monterey Bay Aquarium** in California, visitors are advised to arrive early because of the crowds. Long before opening time, people can be seen milling around the front entrance. Many do not speak English. Most don't know where to go or what to do. Signs are inadequate and cryptically written in only one language. Yet no official from the facility is available to point people toward the end of the queue, discuss specific features of the facility, or answer any other question that might arise. It is a confusing, annoying, and unnecessary atmosphere. Kids get cranky and seniors get tired; parents become impatient; and most everybody becomes exasperated. Based on the mumbling that can be heard in the crowd, strong negative impressions about the aquarium are being formed before people are even allowed through the front gate.

By contrast, at the **Mammoth Mountain Ski Area—** also in California—a specially uniformed corps of hosts is posted from the parking lots to the repair shops to greet the earliest arriving skiers. Everyone gets a cheery hello and a brief comment on conditions. The hosts can be approached to answer questions and deliver assistance long before the ticket booths are open, the restaurants are serving, or the chair lifts are operating. If nothing else, the hosts make visitors feel cared for. There is no anxiety about being in the wrong place or losing time. Based on the favorable comments heard about the service, skiers have been given yet another reason to recommend Mammoth over other western ski resorts.

There is a simple point here. Both the Monterey Aquarium and Mammoth Mountain attract large crowds. The former facility seems to have paid little attention to the full customer experience and, as a result, fosters negative word of mouth comments; Mammoth Mountain, on the other hand, has exceeded customers' expectations and can hope for positive word of mouth commentary.

How successful are *you* at stimulating positive word of mouth comments? Have you been attracting *new* customers or driving *old* ones away? Your response to the following six basic questions will give you an idea of how you stand on these matters:

- Are you really *listening* to what customers are saying about your products, services, or facilities—and doing something about what you hear?

- Are you carefully *watching* how customers react to these products, services, or facilities—because many customers seldom take the time to verbalize an opinion?

- Are you constantly *probing* customers for ideas on how to improve your business—making sure you correctly heard what they said or accurately observed what they did?

- Are you continually *rewarding* customers for their patronage—encouraging them to talk about the business and to come back?

- Are you honestly *informing* customers about past, present, or prospective activities—making them feel a part of your successes and giving them an understanding of your failures?

- Are you continuously *surprising* customers with fresh approaches to old situations—jarring even the most taciturn customer into becoming a spokesperson for the business?

Listening, watching, and probing—to learn how best to stimulate positive word of mouth advertising and limit negative comments—are of little benefit if the business itself then fails to react. Once you have discerned an opportunity or uncovered a problem, you must change a procedure, correct an error, add a facility, give a reward, or share information. For example, you can give your customers a stake in the success of your business by asking for their help. You can also empower your best customers to offer *their* friends, relatives, and associates a discount, gift, or special service on your behalf to create more meaningful conversations about your business.

Contrary to what most people may believe, word of mouth promotion does not occur spontaneously; it happens because it is *stimulated* by something that proves to be:

UNUSUAL
SPECIAL
MEMORABLE
or
DIFFERENT

In short, word of mouth promotions can only flourish when a product, service, or activity is made to be **REMARKABLE**.

> *If you rushed passed the word "remarkable," please just take a moment to look at it again. Decode it as a second grader might: **re-MARK-able**. Remarkable is something so unusual that it bears noting another time. The dictionary says that it is something "worthy of notice, extraordinary, uncommon."*

But we also know that what is remarkable for one person may not be for another. It depends on what your customer has come to *expect* from your business.^ Take a customer that has to return a defective product. Annoyed or disappointed, the customer can only hope that a replacement will be provided or the money refunded without hassle, delay, or excessive paperwork. But what kind of reaction would be achieved if the product were not only replaced, but a gift certificate were added to compensate for the inconvenience and time involved? Do you think this customer might "tell a friend"—as one supermarket chain asks its customers to do?

This book, then, is a **starter kit** of hundreds of ideas and thoughts that can help business people find ways to stimulate and sustain *positive* word of mouth promotion and limit *negative* comments through activities that are worthy of notice, extraordinary, and uncommon!

**PICTURE
THESE
IDEAS
AND
TALK
ABOUT
THESE
*THOUGHTS***

Nearly all
efforts—
to stimulate and sustain
positive word of mouth promotion
and to limit and reduce
negative word of mouth commentary—
fall within the framework of
six basic themes.

These six themes and
the ideas and thoughts
associated with them are
headlined
and
highlighted
on the next two pages.
Details appear
in the remainder
of this section.

Use and adapt these ideas and thoughts
to generate the changes
that will make your
business—in the terms of one
famous newspaper column—
the talk of the town.^

BASIC WORD OF MOUTH THEMES

LISTEN
YOUR CUSTOMERS
ARE
COMMUNICATING

REWARD
YOUR CUSTOMERS
DESERVE
RECOGNITION

WATCH
YOUR CUSTOMERS
ARE
REACTING

INFORM
YOUR CUSTOMERS ARE
PART OF
YOUR BUSINESS

PROBE
YOUR CUSTOMERS
HAVE
IDEAS

SURPRISE
YOUR CUSTOMERS
TALK ABOUT
FRESH APPROACHES

ESSENTIALS OF WORD OF MOUTH PROMOTION

- *Empower* your best customers to award special discounts, services, or privileges to *their* friends, relatives, and associates.

- Provide an array of special *gifts* associated with your business to your customers to send or present to *their* friends, relatives, and associates.

- Assist your customers with useful *information*—directions, advice, some humor, or a new cost- or time saving idea—to share with *their* friends, relatives and associates.

- Give your customers *samples* of your products or aspects of your services to enjoy from time to time.

- Be especially *generous* when asking customers to help you resolve a question, rectify an error, correct a problem, or provide a favor.

- Ask your satisfied customers to serve as a *resource* for others when your company is under consideration to supply a product or provide a service.

- Pay attention to what *kids* and other non-spenders like—they may not buy themselves, but they can talk a lot to their parents and others.

- Use *non-oral techniques*—pictures on a wall, letters in a publication, postcards mailed for free—to substitute and/or encourage personal conversation.

LISTEN
YOUR CUSTOMERS ARE COMMUNICATING

I'LL LET SOMEONE KNOW

GET ME MY AGENT

¿HABLA INGLES?

KIDS ARE PEOPLE, TOO

ONE MINUTE
TO CURTAIN

THE PEN IS MIGHTIER...

HOW TO ATTRACT A MAN—
AND GET A COMMITMENT

DOES THE LEFT HAND KNOW
WHAT THE RIGHT IS UP TO?

"BE ALL THAT YOU CAN BE"—
AND OTHER SUCH PROMISES

I'LL LET SOMEONE KNOW

Complaints and suggestions are often heard by people too low in the decision chain to do anything about them.

A tourist returning his rented car complains to the check-in clerk that the road signs were useless—directions to the airport appear at one intersection but are nowhere to be seen when the road branches later on. A patron in a restaurant specifically asks for White Zinfandel only to be brought Chardonnay "because that's all we carry." The cashier at the hotel says that she hopes the guest had a nice stay and then hears the guest mumble something about "[a]the lousy reading lights in the room."

None of these comments is new or unusual. In fact, most of what ends up as *negative* word of mouth commentary starts to take form at the first opportunity to express dissatisfaction to *someone*. If it can be dealt with immediately and effectively, customers not only may be satisfied, but they can be impressed enough to reverse the negative feelings and talk *positively* about their experience.

The problem is that the recipient of a complaint or a suggestion is usually at the lowest end of the decision chain, with no authority to do anything with the comment made. Moreover, most businesses do not have an immediate, effective, and rewarding *way* to make sure that customer-generated information is moved upward where problems can be solved and ideas can be implemented.

All organizations should push decision authority to resolve complaints or respond to suggestions as low in the chain of command as possible. Some do. For example, both Avis and SAS encourage their employees to try to fix customer problems on the spot; Nordstrom, the

Seattle-based apparel and accessories retailer, tells its employees: "If it makes sense, do it!"^ But, unfortunately, few other companies of any size are equally adept at implementing customer *suggestions* at lower organizational levels.^

Larger organizations should assign someone to field suggestions and complaints and suggestions or install a hot line telephone attached to a dedicated answering machine for the purpose. In either case, the key is to make sure the customers knows that their complaint or suggestion has been *heard* and that the company is grateful for the input.^ Complaints or suggestions handled in this way are then dealt with by someone in authority in an orderly manner and better tracked to see if they occur more than once.

Management should reward employees who pass along customer complaints or suggestions whether or not any changes are implemented.

POINT: *Most customers tend to express their reactions to negative treatment while generally remaining silent about treatment that meets their expectations. As a result, those interested in benefiting from word of mouth promotion need to focus on correcting negative impressions and exceeding the customers' expectations in order to stimulate positive comments.*

GET ME MY AGENT

Literally every business, not just some professions, can benefit from having an agent pushing its interests.

Very few businesses are so vertically integrated that they can survive all by themselves. On the contrary, nearly all businesses are dependent on a roster of suppliers, supporters, and others to provide goods and services needed to conduct their activities. These suppliers, supporters, and others can communicate with prospective customers on your behalf, as well as obtain useful data for you about your products and services from these customers.

We don't think that this amount of *interdependence* is appreciated by everyone in the marketplace. Yet it doesn't take a World Bank economist to realize that the salaries a law firm pays its secretarial staff are, in part, dependent on providing good service to a corporate client and that the client's growth can add to the law firm's success. For the law firm, helping to support the commercial interests of *its* client is not unlike what a literary agent does for an author in his or her talent pool.

In terms of word of mouth promotion, we think the concept of *agentry* can be used to each business's advantage. We believe that every employee of every supplier and supporter can be enlisted as an agent. For example:

- What if a business provided the drivers of its long haul transportation carrier with *special* gifts to be given to other drivers, waitresses at truck stops, employees of motels, and others encountered along the road? We have in mind unique samples of the firm's products and/or germane ad specialty items—outdoor thermometers from fuel oil companies; ice cream scoops from dairies; key rings from security companies—anything other than the ubiquitous T-shirts, caps, calendars, and coffee mugs.

- What if the employees of an insurance agency, for example, had samples of their clients' wares or special discount coupons to distribute to their friends, relatives, and associates, as well as to the other clients of their agency?

- What if the basic business paid or granted other rewards for whenever an "agent's" talk led to a new customer's expenditure?

Costly? It always depends on how one looks at cost. Ad specialty items such as erasable slate pads to carry in a car or truck—to jot down a telephone number or to give to kids to occupy them—may cost $.10 each. But they may be a lot cheaper than a radio ad and a lot more effective in reminding people of the business and its products than a yellow page ad.

POINT: The appreciation and surprise of the recipient for whatever is given away by the "agent" can create the type of conversations about the basic company's products or services that make positive word of mouth promotion so effective.

¿HABLA INGLES?

*Language problems
are a fact of business,
but not part of
business planning or
employee training.*

Since 1975, millions have entered the United States looking for greater economic opportunities. Many have struggled to master English. Often those with the greatest language difficulties are in the closest direct contact with a business's customers—operating taxis, cleaning rooms, carrying equipment, serving in restaurants, selling in stores, and so on.

But, too often, these employees get the least amount of training from their employers—perhaps employees don't speak English well enough to apply for the training; perhaps employers fear they will leave as soon as some other better paying job comes along; perhaps employers don't want them to get ahead; perhaps some think they can't absorb new skills; or perhaps they can't be spared from their regular tasks. We don't know what the answer is, but we would argue that business executives and entrepreneurs ought to take another look at training their bottom level employees on how to service customers.

Aren't these the people likely to make a major impression on the customer? Shouldn't they be given a good command of the language just to be able to communicate better with the customers? Shouldn't they also know some elementary facts about how the business operates, where things are located, what the company's goals are, who does what within the organization, and how to help customers solve problems? We think so. We also think businesses should learn the rudiments of languages spoken by their customers, no matter the seeming difficulty. For us, this holds equally true for Anglo businesses that suddenly find themselves serving new Russian immigrants or for

Iranian-owned stores located in, say, a Korean neighborhood.

POINT: *To generate solid word of mouth commentary, businesses need to see themselves as a whole—that no matter how and where a customer comes into contact with any of their employees or facilities, the customer will be well and carefully treated. Put another way, everyone in every enterprise needs to be involved in marketing and customer service.^*

You have to be able to deal with all
kinds of customers.

KIDS ARE PEOPLE, TOO

*When kids talk—
and they do—
their parents and
other kids listen.*

A number of businesses pay special attention to their younger patrons—airlines award wings; restaurants provide games; shoe stores give out candy; and medical offices offer toys. Most of this special attention is designed to keep the kids *occupied*.

But one should also remember that kids can be very *verbal*. It may well be that kids talk a lot because at their level more things strike them as *remarkable*. They talk among themselves and they talk to their parents. Moreover, what people learn to like as kids often stays with them as adults. Most fast food restaurant chains cater special promotions to their smaller patrons. If you treat the kids in ways that *they* appreciate, they tell their friends about where they went and what they did. They also ask their parents to take them to the same place again.

Always remember kids are people, too. Talk to them about what they like and don't like. Listen to what they want and don't want. Don't guess and don't presume that you can make choices for them. Ask teachers, psychologists, and other professionals to assist, when appropriate. But having asked kids for their opinions, also make sure that they aren't asking for things their parents might object to.

POINT: In designing a word of mouth program, listen to those most likely to talk to others. Focus attention on them even if they aren't the money-spending customers. Kids, guests, observers, reporters, and others can make good spokespersons.

LISTEN
YOUR CUSTOMERS ARE COMMUNICATING

ONE MINUTE TO CURTAIN

Eavesdropping, although distasteful to some, is an important source for understanding what customers talk about.

Both directors and producers have been known to lurk in the foyer of theaters to listen surreptitiously to what people say to each other about a movie, play, or concert during intermissions or at the end of a performance. Somehow, the intimacy and immediacy of such conversations yield the kind of honest, raw, and basic feelings that help producers and directors adjust their shows to the likes and dislikes of their audiences. The same kind of adjustments, when made to products, services, or activities, can be crucial to encouraging positive word of mouth comments and limiting negative ones. The next time you're in line at the bank, post office, or supermarket, listen to the conversations and ruminations of the people around you.^ It is word of mouth commentary at the instant of creation that may help you in your business.^

There is another point here. Many products, services, or events are imminently forgettable—so bland that people have *nothing* positive or negative to say about them. When that is the case, little of use will be overheard. Because of this phenomena, eavesdropping may serve as a better indicator of the *impact* of any product, service, or event than most other methods available. Asked to evaluate something in a survey or focus group, for example, most people can find something to remember or fib sufficiently well to avoid embarrassment—but it may not be the *truth* about their feelings.

POINT: *There are many opportunities for eavesdropping. Use them. But also remember that companies that have products or services that blend into the background of everyday life will not be able to take advantage of promoting their businesses through word of mouth.*

LISTEN
YOUR CUSTOMERS ARE COMMUNICATING

THE PEN IS MIGHTIER...

Not all word of mouth commentary is spread orally; some of the most important comments may be written.

Political groups learned long ago that politicians are sensitive to their mail. But getting people to write letters today, even when they feel passionately on a subject, is sometimes hard. Hence, the development of *form* letters. You've seen them in every newspaper. Readers are urged to clip something out, put it in an envelope addressed to the White House or some congressional office, and mail it. Even if the political staffs do nothing more than *count* the incoming forms, they have an idea of the depth of feeling about a particular issue.

Political campaigns have taken to using the same technique. But now supporters of individual candidates or issues are being given *preprinted* postcards. Here's one, designed to be sent to friends, on a 1990 California issue:

> *I want to reform our government, but I think spending millions of hard earned taxpayers dollars on...politicians' campaigns is a waste. Please vote against Proposition 131.*

The proposition lost. There were many reasons for a negative vote, of course, but the cards were certainly one factor. They are also a way of institutionalizing word of mouth commentary. They work almost the same way as conversation—offering the power and personal credibility that conversation affords, but allowing more precision on complicated topics as a uniform message passes from friend to friend.

Any business can do the same thing. Preprint a message about your services or products on stamped postcards and leave them around for patrons to complete and address to friends. If an issue affecting your business arises in the newspaper or on television, consider writing a letter to the editor or news director to stimulate word of mouth comments in support of your position.

POINT: *Postcards, other preprinted messages, and letters to the editor are something sure to cause comment between the sender and recipient or a writer and reader at some later time. If that conversation yields one more paying customer, the effort may well prove to have been worth it.*

LISTEN
YOUR CUSTOMERS ARE COMMUNICATING

HOW TO ATTRACT A MAN— AND GET A COMMITMENT

Embarrassing topics can also be the focus of word of mouth campaigns.

Single women in Los Angeles have long been attending a seminar sponsored by The Female Connection called *How to Attract a Man—and Get a Commitment.* For many, it is a subject they think they shouldn't have to be taught. But the fact is that some women simply don't know how or where to meet men. Others, even though they seem to find men, have trouble getting a permanent relationship with them. It is also one of those products or services seldom discussed among friends, relatives, or associates.

It isn't the product or service so much as the *subject* that seems to put discussions off limits. Incontinence among the elderly may be another one of these untouchables; hemorrhoids can be another.

To stimulate word of mouth promotion of her seminars, the owner of The Female Connection substantially discounts her fees when women sign up in *pairs.* Coming together gives many the courage they need to attend and the incentive of the savings encourages them to broach a sensitive subject to others. The owner has also given rebates for referrals from past participants and asked her success stories—those who found and married men using her techniques—to talk about their experiences with those who need encouragement to sign up.^

POINT: *A topic that may be embarrassing doesn't mean that businesses offering products or services dealing with these areas are without ways to stimulate and sustain some kind of word of mouth commentary.*

DOES THE LEFT HAND KNOW WHAT THE RIGHT IS UP TO?

Nothing sets off negative word of mouth commentary quite as quickly as when a major company looks foolish in the eyes of its customers.

Not very long ago a client asked us to arrange to have all of his considerable accounts—business, personal, loans, securities—moved from a major money center bank to a smaller institution.

It seems his money center bank had purchased several large U.S. Treasury bills for him. When one of the bills came due, the bank's in-house securities dealer redeemed the certificate and sent the funds for deposit to the customer's business account at a branch of the *same* bank. About two weeks later, federal rates turned up, and the customer decided to buy another T-Bill. He placed the order with the bank's securities firm, and they in turn debited his business account for the purchase price. But this time the bank's computer balked. *It* never recorded the first deposit, so *it* couldn't honor the payment request. Instead, it issued a Not Sufficient Funds notice to its own subsidiary and notified our client that he was being debited $10.00.

It took awhile, but after a number of letters, photocopies of the records generated, and some exasperated phone calls, the matter was clarified. The client was given a credit for the $10. But he hasn't stopped talking about it. The bank looked foolish. Far worse from our perspective, though, the bank made a major error in not foreseeing the potential word of mouth damage that the episode might cause. Had they issued an apology, explained what had happened, given the client a high-level assurance of corrective action to prevent similar problems in the future, it might have been sufficient to end the negative word of mouth commentary from spreading. But they didn't!

Had the bank gone one small step further—and apologized in the form of a free year's dues on the client's credit card membership, a free year's safety deposit fees, even sending some postage paid envelopes for his mail deposits—it could have turned potentially negative comments into enthusiastic positive support. Another major bank has done just that. First Interstate Bank advertises that if a customer finds that the bank has made an error, the customer receives $5 on the spot. In one fell swoop, this bank turns potentially negative comments into something the customer will probably later brag about to friends, relatives, and associates.

As *The Wall St. Journal* has noted: " Apologies have all but disappeared from America's commercial discourse..." * They cite the litigation explosion and a diminishing sense of personal responsibility for the mistakes made by others within a large company as the reasons.

POINT: *It's possible to convert a mistake into a benefit with a sincere apology and a touch of generosity.*

"I really apologize. If we ever get out of here, you'll all get free rides for a month."

LISTEN
YOUR CUSTOMERS ARE COMMUNICATING

Advertisements that offer more than can be delivered or convey unfortunate messages are the breeding ground for negative word of mouth advertising.

"BE ALL THAT YOU CAN BE"— AND OTHER SUCH PROMISES

The U.S. military has been selling everything *but* the possibility that its volunteer recruits may be used in hostilities. With the advent of the Persian Gulf War in January 1991, a lot of young people realized for the first time that the military could be more than a "good place to start," "an adventure," "a way to earn money for college," and other such safe upbeat themes.^ By the same token, a well-known diet suppressant—called AYDS—seemed to be popular until the name came to be associated with Acquired Immune Deficiency Syndrome.

No institution can fully predict how its name or advertising message may be interpreted as times, events, and language evolve, but every institution ought to be flexible enough to adjust to those changes as they occur whenever expectations differ from reality.

If it isn't, it may become a prime target for the late night television comedians. Once a product or service opens itself to ridicule, it suffers from the most punishing form of negative word of mouth commentary. Good jokes zoom from person to person on the phone, through interoffice Xeroxes, on E-mail networks, and via FAXes to distant locations.

POINT: *Positive word of mouth comments can only begin when the public believes that a company's products are good and the messages it sponsors are accurate, honest, and sincere. Remember what Vice President Walter Mondale used to say: "[images are like] mixing cement. When its wet, you can move it around and mold it; but at some point it hardens and there's almost nothing you can do to reshape it."*

To Review

LISTEN
YOUR CUSTOMERS ARE COMMUNICATING

Customers are continually communicating with business people about the products and services they are sold. Sometimes they communicate verbally, sometimes not. Whatever way the messages are delivered, are they understood? What is done with the information can have an enormous subsequent influence on what people say to one another about those products and services.

KEY POINTS

- *Quickly resolve complaints and respond to suggestions at an organization level visible to the customers so that they know the issue is being addressed.*

- *Visibly reward both employees and customers for communicating the complaints and suggestions they hear or offer.*

- *Train everyone in the organization to become the ears of the company and on how to deal with customer questions, needs, or problems.*

- *Make sure all of your employees, suppliers, and supporters are enlisted as agents to promote your products and services.*

- *Aim your activities at the full customer spectrum—those who spend money directly, those who benefit from others who spend, and those who merely observe.*

- *Look at your business from every angle to make sure your customers perceive it as you do.*

- *Help customers communicate with their friends about your products and services through preprinted cards and other messages.*

- *Compensate customers when rectifying errors and be sure to apologize for the inconvenience caused.*

- *Stay alert to changing factors that alter your customers' expectations and try to deliver more than your customers' expect.*

WATCH
YOUR CUSTOMERS ARE REACTING

WATCH MY HIPS, NOT MY LIPS

TO THE WALL

STAGE RIGHT, PLEASE

USE IT OR LOSE IT

MISERY LOVES COMPANY

HOW DO THEY DO THAT?

DOESN'T ANYBODY KNOW?

WATCH MY HIPS, NOT MY LIPS

Non-verbal communication can convey a lot of information to the observant.

When reporters from the *National Enquirer* were found going through former Secretary of State Henry Kissinger's trash, they said they thought they might find something interesting for their readers. While the Kissinger episode repulsed a number of people in Washington, some saw it as an extension of a Navy effort to find out what foods sailors *really* liked and disliked by studying what was left on mess trays.

How many times have you responded to a waiter's inquiry—"Everything OK here?"—with a perfunctory, "Fine," or a simple nod of the head.^ While this may be an honest reflection of your feelings at the time, it may also be that you simply can't be bothered to go through a litany of comments or complaints: "The potatoes are too greasy," "The portions are uneven," or "The coffee is tepid." You retreat, instead, to a little fib.

But patrons generally won't fib to their friends when describing an experience. Everything they found wrong without telling the business itself can get discussed. Negative word of mouth can be spreading *before* the establishment is even aware of a problem.

Look for non-verbal clues in your own business. The garbage or the contents of "doggy bags"are good clues for restaurants; the way cars move into and around a parking lot is a good indicator of how people view a shopping center; what people notice when entering a store or focus on at a trade show booth helps you make things more visible and accessible. By the same token, people who leave early from an event may be expressing a problem with some of the arrangements.

On the other hand, first time customers who come back to a hotel and old customers who continue to book rooms there are signaling they like something without ever submitting an evaluation form or speaking to an assistant manager. Get them to articulate their reasons for possible use in a future marketing program.

> **POINT:** *To be sure that you are getting a completely honest appraisal of your business from your patrons, look for nonverbal signals as well as spoken comments.*

Pictures on a wall can be as valuable as a verbal recommendation.

TO THE WALL

An ancient proverb has it that one picture is worth a thousand words. That may be no more true of journalism than commerce. Reception area walls in pediatric offices are covered with pictures of happy patients; veterinarians display photos of pets they have helped; the post offices in Encino, California, have a wall of publicity photos of the celebrities it serves—Michael Jackson, Janet Jackson, and many others.

But instead of celebrities and chance snapshots, businesses interested in the power of word of mouth marketing might make an arrangement with a local professional photographer and send favored customers to have their formal portraits done. The customer comes away with a valuable and lasting memento to share with friends and family and the business has another piece of art for its wall of fame.

Just as people recognize celebrities in photos, they also recognize their neighbors. The pictures on the wall become the silent "word of mouth" testimony of the people portrayed, ensure the loyalty and continued patronage of those honored, and can stimulate conversations with others. Wouldn't it be pleasing if your framed portrait were on a wall of the local hardware store—honoring customers for their 5, 10, or 15 years of business—and someone approached you with a question: "Didn't I see your photo in All Things Hardware store?"

POINT: *Honoring your customers with something as visible and as appealing as a Wall of Appreciation is a powerful way to build loyalty and generate word of mouth conversations.*

WATCH
YOUR CUSTOMERS ARE REACTING

STAGE RIGHT, PLEASE

Make sure you see your product from the same angles as your customers see it.

No matter how much effort and rehearsal is put into stage productions destined for the West End of London or Broadway in New York, producers arrange to have the play performed in suburban or out-of-town theaters to make sure that everything works properly. Of late, film studios have taken to the same practice—tinkering with a movie in the editing studio even after formally showing it to selected audiences around the country. Perhaps because dining is often considered entertainment, many restaurants offer free meals while conducting pre-grand-opening practice sessions for their staffs.

What is happening here? Artistic people used to rely on their own professional judgments to decide what is good and bad in any performance. Now they have learned that audiences often react quite differently and in unexpected ways to what they see and hear. Take a stage production. In rehearsal, actors can sharpen their interaction with each other, but until they hear an audience laugh at a line or respond to a scene, their timing will be imperfect. Take the theater itself. A director can position his actors to develop the perfect physical movements, but not until there is an audience can he tell whether the audience can hear what is being said or see everything that is being done. It is a lesson that all actors and all directors have to learn. It is a lesson that all business people need to learn as well.

> **POINT:** *Until you have watched a product in use or observed a service under real-life conditions, you don't really know how it will actually function. Test, practice, rehearse, and review are lessons for all businesses to follow.*

USE IT OR LOSE IT

Make sure that friendly folks use your product continually to keep you informed about how it wears or works in practice.

It is often said that the toughest part of product development is not getting a new idea to work, but getting it to work *reliably*. Like doctors in an emergency room collecting stories about unusual accidents, so repair specialists can tell you about the destruction and mayhem that ordinary people can visit upon otherwise innocent machinery. Spills, drops, and foreign objects are only half of what can ruin a photocopier or wreck a computer. As Murphy might have said: Whatever can be done to a machine will likely be done by someone at some time. The simple truth is that few manufacturers fully understand their products until they have been on the market for a few years.

Managers can take a lesson from this. They need to have their products in use by people who will honestly discuss how the product does over time—what changes are noticed, what weaknesses appear, what benefits can be emphasized—to ensure that corrections are made. Some say don't fix it if it isn't broken; yet we have a hunch that in terms of word of mouth commentary, *complacency* can spoil success more than any other factor.

POINT: Managers ought never stop gathering customer data. Once you have done the best possible job getting a product or service to market, watch it over time to make sure that what you thought you developed is the same item that others observe. There is no time limit on word of mouth commentary. It can start at any moment and be effective in helping or hindering a product, service, or activity in its further development.

WATCH
YOUR CUSTOMERS ARE REACTING

MISERY LOVES COMPANY

Enlist satisfied customers to help prospects overcome their natural fear of the unknown.

In Las Vegas and other gambling resorts, casino operators sometimes employ people called *shills* to stimulate business at the gaming tables. Experience has proven that most casual gamblers don't like to sit by themselves. They think their money goes too fast when they are alone or feel intimidated by the skill of the dealer. To overcome these fears, casinos hire people to play with house money to encourage members of the public to play beside them.

We don't recommend employing shills—in other businesses they might fraudulently convey the illusion of demand. But we do believe in a related concept to stimulate word of mouth advertising. We refer to it as the "Adjunct Consultant." These are customers who are willing to talk with others about their experiences with your business.

Asking your best customers to serve from time to time as consultants to new prospects can be effective in keeping old business in touch and generating new business as well.

POINT: *Unsolicited testimony from a stranger with nothing to gain—but the flattering realization that his expertise is valued—is another form of word of mouth promotion stimulated by a business owner or manager.*

*Becoming your
competitor's customer
gives you the chance
to see the world
through your own
customers' eyes.*

HOW DO THEY DO THAT?

When travel agents *travel* on business, they tend to be coddled by the airlines, receive special attention from host communities, get express services in airports, and enjoy royal treatment by hotels. While obviously very nice for the travel agents, it generally doesn't prove beneficial to their customers. The travel agents do not see the world as most of their customers will see it. The agents' planning, decisions, and advice may well be tainted by the luxuries *they* enjoyed, but which many of their clients can't afford or can't hope to receive.

All business people can learn from this example. Treat yourself as your customers are treated. Every so often become an ordinary customer of a competitor—buying or returning something, asking for help, making a suggestion. When business people operate in foreign camps, they should be attuned to every feeling about how they are treated, carefully observe how various aspects of the business are handled, and ask questions that delve into the policies of their rivals. The Chairman of the QVC Network, for example, is reported to constantly call competitive TV shopping channels to probe for details about the items they are then offering.^

POINT: *Making yourself a guinea pig—with all your senses alive to every aspect of your experience as a customer—can help you understand what people may later talk about. The experience can also help you make changes to improve your own operation and accentuate the differences between the way you conduct your business and the way your competitors conduct theirs.*

WATCH
YOUR CUSTOMERS ARE REACTING

DOESN'T ANYBODY KNOW?

Make someone in your organization responsible for filling the role of institutional memory.

Ask anyone who has ever run a governmental unit about its most valuable employee, and the response usually points to someone who has been around the agency for a generation or more. Often referred to as the institutional memory, these people remember *why* policies were adopted long after the supporting memos have gone into storage and years after the computers have been *applying* the policy in support of the unit's work. Essentially, the institutional memory saves political bosses from looking like they just got off the turnip truck.

Some major enterprises expect their in-house librarians to serve as the institutional memory; small enterprises sometimes look to the boss's secretary. Whatever the case, all enterprises should make a conscious effort to assign one of their employees to the additional task of being in a position to answer and document the historical and procedural (as opposed to the substantive and policy) questions that arise. Not only does a person filling the role of institutional memory make managing easier, he or she can also build the kind of public reputation for the business that causes people to comment to others about how responsive the enterprise is to its customers.

We were reminded of the need for someone with an institutional memory when we visited a large shopping center in search of an immerser—those electrical devices that boil water in a cup. We weren't sure if we should try the drug store, the hardware store, one of the department stores, or the electronics store. We went to the information booth. It was crowded. We soon found out why. The clerk was selling lottery tickets at a time when the prize was substantial. When we got our turn, she was not only unhappy we didn't want a lottery ticket, she also didn't have a clue where the item we needed might be found. Worse, she didn't even have a *suggestion* of where we might start our inquiry. We left the center annoyed and disappointed.

By now, many of us are inured to this sort of treatment. In fact, some may *expect* it. But that is our point. Put someone with brains, charm, and an interest in helping people in an information booth, and startled customers may soon *talk* about the treatment received. While getting someone with talent may cost a little more, it may turn out to be one of the least costly *advertising* expenses incurred during a year.

POINT: *Appoint someone in your organization to serve as the principal information source and institutional memory and get that person to assemble the organization's historical archives and current encyclopedia of facts—a place where the history of the operation and a classified directory of activities can be kept in one place and easily accessed when needed.*

The Standard in
Institutional Memory

To Review

WATCH
YOUR CUSTOMERS ARE REACTING

Clues as to what people may say to others about a product or service—both favorably and unfavorably—can sometimes be determined from observing customer movements, as well as from becoming a customer yourself. People may not always *tell* the truth, but their physical reactions may describe what they really *feel is* the truth.

KEY POINTS

- *Remember that non-verbal clues are important in learning what customers may really think about your products or services.*

- *Use photos on the wall—or other visual symbols—to suggest that others would speak favorably of your products or services if they were available for a conversation.*

- *Check on how your product works or your service is perceived in practice and over time.*

- *Understand how your customers are seeing and using your product.*

- *Ask good customers to serve as advisors to the prospects to whom you wish to sell your products or services.*

- *Put yourself in the position of your customers as often as possible to experience what they experience when dealing with your business.*

- *Make sure at least one person in your operation specializes in helping customers find where things are and in describing how things used to be in your organization.*

PROBE
YOUR CUSTOMERS
HAVE IDEAS

**GET 'EM TOGETHER
AND YOU'LL GET 'EM TALKING**

**THERE'S NO BUSINESS LIKE
SHOW BUSINESS**

GOOD EYE, BATTER

**LET'S PUT A FAX MACHINE IN
EVERY ROOM**

ASK AND YE SHALL RECEIVE

SILENCE MAY NOT BE GOLDEN

**REFERENCES AVAILABLE ON
REQUEST**

**NEGATIVE TIME IS
WASTED TIME**

SAVING GRACE

**TREAT CUSTOMERS AS YOU WOULD
WANT TO BE TREATED**

Focus groups are one of the more effective ways of learning about public attitudes toward products, services, or facilities.

GET 'EM TOGETHER AND YOU'LL GET 'EM TALKING

Stay in a hotel belonging to any major chain and you will find a questionnaire in a drawer probing you on the service and conditions you found. How many people ever fill these out? What happens to the survey forms—are they ever *read* for their comments or merely scanned into a computer?^ Get on any airline about a month before the quarter ends and accept the fact that the flight attendant may be asking you to participate in a marketing survey: "Was the reservation for this trip made by [check one]: ❑ you, ❑ an employee, ❑ a travel agent, ❑ a family member?" Be home at dinner time during the work week and the phone is sure to ring with yet another public opinion survey—for a local supermarket trying to determine whether to issue a private credit card, a political candidate deciding what issues to emphasize, or some other entity trying to learn what the public may want.

We think many establishments can start positive word of mouth comments and learn things to improve their products or services in the process by randomly creating *discussion groups* among their clientele. Regularly invite a few people to discuss ideas with you or a staff member in comfortable surroundings; make sure that your guests are handsomely rewarded for their participation—with honoraria, drinks, food, special assistance, and/or gifts; establish an atmosphere in which participants are encouraged to be honest; ask questions that will help you understand what they like and dislike about your activities by digging gently to get to bottom line *feelings*; and, most of all, listen carefully to what people say when they speak and try hard not to be defensive in justifying the company's attitudes.

Focus groups—whether informally formed by in-house staff or scientifically created by outside consultants—are invaluable for understanding customer perceptions about a business or product. Moreover, in listening and watching how customers interact with each other, managers are witness to the creation of word of mouth comments about their business and products.

POINT: *Focus groups can cut two ways. They can be enormously useful in co-opting your patrons into becoming your virtual partners in the enterprise—taking pride in your success, talking about their experiences, feeling "ownership" in changes made. They can also be counter-productive—if the business proves defensive or non-objective or uses the group to sell participants something rather than simply to elicit information from them.*

Everyone enjoys focus groups.

THERE'S NO BUSINESS
LIKE SHOW BUSINESS

*There has to be
a little bit of
show business in
every other business.*

One of the most impressive things about theatrical productions is that audiences are usually unable to distinguish the performance they see from the one given on opening night. No matter how many times a professional cast does a show, the intensity, the energy, and the craftsmanship always seem to remain at a high level.^

Businesses can adopt the same ethic, whether selling something on a show room floor, answering the phone, responding to a piece of mail, or dealing with the public in some other way. For the customer, it may be the first time to ask a question, seek help, or acquire some product or service. For the employee, however, it may be the umpteenth time to respond to an inquiry. No matter. How the customer is handled is the way *that* customer will talk about the business and the treatment received to relatives, friends, and associates. Neiman Marcus is conscious of this principle. It has a rule that customers must be greeted within 90 seconds of crossing a department threshold. A supermarket chain in Southern California has a sign at the exit of its employee lounge that reads simply: "Show Time." Probe your first time customers soon after they deal with your employees on their impressions. Quiz older customers on how they have been treated by employees immediately after an encounter. You'd be surprised how a little reward or reprimand for employees—when either is necessary—maintains a high level of service that yields the kind of comments that can bring new business.

POINT: *To make sure your employees are up and on stage when dealing with the public test them from time to time with the kind of repetitive inquiries that they are continually answering.*

PROBE
YOUR CUSTOMERS HAVE IDEAS

GOOD EYE, BATTER

New people tend to see things through fresh eyes; old hands see things as part of the woodwork.

At the American Embassy in London a few years ago, the elevators gave no clue to determine how the floors were designated. While most Americans assumed that they would reach the main entrance on the ground floor by pressing "1," the English expected "1" to be the first floor *above* the ground floor. When people used the elevators for the first time, they were confused by which system was being employed. But once visitors had sorted out for themselves the way the floors were designated, that person never gave the matter another thought.

As a result, the confusion about the floors existed for years until the Counselor of Embassy for Administration happened to interview a newly arrived assistant to the Ambassador about his initial impressions of the Embassy. That officer, fresh from Washington, mentioned the elevator confusion. No one had ever asked this kind of question of newly arrived personnel before. The Counselor understood the problem and immediately ordered little plaques placed next to each button to explain the floor numbering system. Soon thereafter, a pattern was established so that *all* new personnel were asked about *their* first impressions of the Embassy on a wide range of matters.

POINT: *Find a way to capture people's first impressions at the instant they occur; like dreams, the specifics of a first impression tend to be forgotten, but the feelings persist. And it is often first impressions that become the foundation for everything else that makes people talk about an enterprise. As has been sagely noted by others: "You never get a second chance to make a first impression."*

LET'S PUT A FAX IN EVERY ROOM

*Asking hotel guests what they might like—and prompting them with possibilities—can be revealing.^*

Most written questionnaires are not flexible enough to probe for details that would make your business sufficiently different to prompt word of mouth commentary. Even when questionnaires get specific, they tend to be like the list of diseases on a life insurance application—too long to want to bother with voluntarily. Why should anyone fill out these questionnaires? What incentive is there for respondents to be totally honest? More significantly, how do you compare the value of one respondent's ideas with another's on an anonymous questionnaire? In lieu of a questionnaires, many car dealers have taken to calling customers for their views on the quality of the service they received from their mechanics and managers.^

To get ideas on which patrons *really* think what, it is valuable for top executives and managers to get up from behind their desks and speak with their customers. Alternatively, they can be put in touch with customers by phone. It isn't a focus group, but it attains some of the same ends. While direct contact with the customer is scary for many managers, they often benefit greatly from learning personally what customers like and dislike, and the customer feels flattered at having been asked.

POINT: *There is great value when the person probing for information and reactions is someone who can make the decisions to implement the ideas received or correct the problems expressed. Customers involved tend to take a protective view toward the business, and can become important vehicles for spreading word of mouth comments.*

PROBE
YOUR CUSTOMERS HAVE IDEAS

ASK AND YE SHALL RECEIVE

If you have the courage to ask the right questions, you'll get the answers you need to get people talking about your products or services.

One of the great stories of entrepreneurial success in the 1980s revolves around the Zagat Restaurant Surveys. The story goes that Mr. Zagat was a New York lawyer and that he and his wife ate out often. They fell into the habit of making notes on the restaurants after each meal: what they had liked, disliked, paid, and so forth. Before long, their friends took to calling the Zagats for information about various restaurants. Things got to the point that the Zagats decided to send a Xeroxed listing of all their comments on Manhattan restaurants to their friends at Christmas time. Pretty soon the friends were contributing their own thoughts on the restaurants the Zagats had visited and adding new ones for the Zagats to try.

Eventually the job got so large and complex that the Zagats decided to print their list and invite anyone to submit an opinion. Soon Mr. Zagat stopped practicing law to devote full time to his publication business. Now he has gone well beyond New York to other cities. The 1991 Los Angeles guide, for example, is a compilation of the views of some 3,000 people who consumed approximately 500,000 meals.

Unlike professional restaurant critics—who may sample one or two dishes at a restaurant on a single visit every few years—the Zagat Restaurant Surveys are effective because the ratings are based on thousands of meals eaten over a year-long period by multitudes of restaurant goers.^ In effect, the Zagats found a way to *institutionalize* word of mouth commentary. They have compiled what people say to each other about restaurants for the benefit and appreciation of all.

A Zagat-style book covering *Hollywood talent agents*—featuring the comments of actors on the agents listed—is widely used by other actors and entertainment professionals looking for representation.

POINT: *With a little thought, anyone can create a similar listing that institutionalizes word of mouth comments and information about the principal players in a particular field. The subject isn't as important as the format in which the information is developed. Asking the right questions gets honest answers—the kind of answers that are the basis of word of mouth comments. The truth does indeed sometimes hurt, but as it is the basis of freedom, so it may well be the difference between the ultimate success and failure of any business.*

PROBE
YOUR CUSTOMERS HAVE IDEAS

SILENCE MAY NOT BE GOLDEN

*Many people are simply reluctant to share their thoughts with strangers— even though they may act on those thoughts.^*

Friends of ours were living in an apartment when the pipes in a neighboring unit burst. The mess was staggering. The owners immediately relocated all tenants to a nearby hotel until repairs to the damaged floors and walls could be completed. We went to visit our friends and were impressed with what appeared to us to be the first class hotel accommodations provided by their landlord.

"Not really," the wife said, "the bed is awful." Even though they were in what appeared to be a comfortable suite, she complained that every morning she awoke with a terrible backache. She longed to be back in her own apartment. "Have you mentioned the bed problem to the hotel's management?" we asked. When she indicated no, we said we were sure that they would be glad to change the mattress or find another room. We surmised from her reaction to our suggestion that she didn't want to complain, didn't want to appear to be a nuisance, didn't want to be counted as a troublemaker, and most of all didn't want to spend the energy necessary to get the problem resolved. But the interesting thing was that the same hotel chain expected to open additional facilities in other parts of the state. "Ugh," said the wife. "I'd never stay at another one." The bed problem had now infected her total perception of the business.

Sometimes negative word of mouth is unfair, inaccurate, or malicious. But just as innocent people find themselves victimized by crimes or terrorists, so businesses have to be aware that negative word of mouth commentary can sometimes start from the least suspected sources and for totally unknown reasons. Be aware. The only thing a business can do is plan for the worst and never be complacent.

POINT: *Invent ways to get even the shy and the recalcitrant to express themselves. One way is to work on asking questions that produce useful answers, rather than questions that fill space.^*

Try:

- *What could we do to make your visit better the next time you are with us?*

Avoid:

- *How is everything?*

*In addition, reward customers with food, drink, or gifts if they participate in helping improve service, products, or facilities. Word of mouth, it must be noted, is not a testimonial. Anyone who expresses himself or herself can do the same amount of good or harm; in word of mouth advertising, everyone is **equal**.*

PROBE
YOUR CUSTOMERS HAVE IDEAS

REFERENCES AVAILABLE
UPON REQUEST

*Probing for a reference
from a satisfied customer
can be a good substitute for
direct conversation.*

The world is a busy place; all of us have our own concerns. The older each of us gets, the fewer hours seem available to do all the things we would like to do or to meet all the obligations we have accumulated over the years. As a result, it is no surprise to realize that not everyone finds the time or energy to get into discussions with friends, relatives, or associates about a company's products, services, or facilities.

Conversations take time; it is hard to get on and off a phone or in and out of a conversation at a party. There is an American social convention that personal notes ought to be shared before any business topics can be raised. We believe this convention is one reason message machines and the FAX have become so popular. They not only leave a record of the thoughts transmitted, they allow the people communicating to get directly to the business point at hand without seeming rude.

Because of these factors, rather than rely solely on your customers to tout your business or product to their friends, we suggest that you probe each satisfied customer or client for the name and address of someone they know who might appreciate learning about what your business offers. Then a subsequent letter, FAX communication, or phone call from you to the referred person can begin with those appealing words: "Mr. (or Ms.)_____ suggested that I be in touch with you about..."

We recently received a full-color printed greeting card from the sales manager of our automobile leasing company with the legend: "I Welcome Your Referrals!" It struck us as a bit cold and formal. Doesn't it make sense that if you want others to talk for *you*, you should talk to *them* first? Worse, the card was accompanied by a stuffer that asked recipients to list the referrals they had made for the leasing company. "Any referral that becomes a lease can earn an easy $100 for you." While we would agree that asking others to help you deserves some kind of reward, anything that sounds so crassly mercenary will probably be counter-productive. We suggest that the psychological reward of doing someone else a favor, the expectation of having something reciprocal done for you, or the surprise inherent in receiving a gift by way of thanks may be enough to generate effective word of mouth promotional help.

> *POINT: Personally ask satisfied customers or clients for referrals. If you don't think they will be inclined to speak to a friend, relative, or associate on your behalf, then their recommendation may be the next best thing to simulate the power of word of mouth promotion.*^

PROBE
YOUR CUSTOMERS HAVE IDEAS

NEGATIVE TIME IS
WASTED TIME!

Going over something that you thought had been settled can create the worst kind of negative word of mouth commentary.

You paid the bill last month, but you get another invoice from the company "gently reminding" you of the serious consequences of being delinquent. Do you call or assume they'll eventually discover that you paid? A second order comes in from a client identical to the first one you already filled. Is this a new order or did they forget that they had already ordered the item? Fill it and you may be hassling with returns; ignore it and you may be explaining why your client service is so shoddy.

Negative time is the amount of time spent on solving problems that *you* thought had already been solved or resolving issues *you* didn't think needed resolving. For example, hunting for a receipt to demonstrate to the IRS that a deduction was legitimate; chasing or suing a customer for failing to pay a valid charge for a product or service you provided; searching for a cancelled check to show that the company had already taken your money for the service rendered; retracing your steps to get duplicate documents because something was "misplaced" or "lost in the mail."

We once thought about how much advancement we could all provide society if none of us ever had to spend negative time. It is a daydream, of course. The more complex our society becomes, the more crowded our lives, the more likely that we will be spending increasing amounts of negative time.

Getting your customers involved in solving a problem—in short, spending negative time—may be the only way for a business to proceed. Just remember to be sensitive to the imposition you have made on your customer. Should it turn out that the business was in error after probing the client for information, make amends to the customer in the most generous sort of way. If the customer turns out to have been wrong when probed, the business still needs to appreciate the assistance in settling the matter.

> **POINT:** *You can turn negative time into a positive benefit—and expect work of mouth comments to result—by being especially generous with customers who are asked for assistance.*

Maybe our *customers* will know what to do.

PROBE
YOUR CUSTOMERS HAVE IDEAS

SAVING GRACE

Most people don't look for ways to express negative impressions.

When managers hear or learn of negative comments, they can be thankful for one thing: most people who have a bad experience with a product or service aren't looking to get revenge; they generally won't lead a crusade against the product or a company. While some will talk to their friends, relatives, or associates about a bad experience, it may end there. While the damage has been done, it may not spread.

But knowing this, a business cannot ignore the problem expressed in the negative comments.^ They must deal with it lest a single problem becomes a pattern—and patterns are what develop a reputation. While a favorable reputation is hard to develop, a poor reputation is almost impossible to reverse.

As a result, any negative comments heard should serve as a firm's early warning system—an over-the-horizon radar signal to indicate the *possibility* of a pending danger without necessarily indicating an imminent disaster. Once a problem identified by a negative comment is corrected, let the customer know of the change and at the same time probe to be sure that there is nothing else that needs fixing.

> POINT: *While it is comforting to know that negative comments may not result in losses or a spreading campaign of destruction for a business or product, they cannot be ignored either. To do so is to put your operation in further peril. Use negative word of mouth feedback to correct the problems identified.*

TREAT CUSTOMERS AS YOU WOULD WANT TO BE TREATED

Adapting the Golden Rule to business makes as much sense as adopting it for personal matters.

A year ago, DHL World Wide Express notified us of an invoice it said was overdue. We knew we had paid that bill and assumed DHL would discover that fact. But a month or so later, we were told our future business would be refused if the bill were not paid. This time we sent a letter *and* a copy of both sides of the cancelled check. Two months later, we were informed by a collection agency that they had the account and would prosecute us if the bill went unpaid. Exasperated, we sent *them* a new letter, along with a copy of the first one *and* its enclosures. We heard nothing further until we needed a package picked up for delivery overseas. When we called, DHL showed our account in arrears. We explained. They said they would investigate.

Four hours later, word came back that the package would be collected. We said it would be nice to receive a written acknowledgment from the company or the collection agency that the matter had been closed. We have never heard a word. As a result, we have kept our file open, our copies of the check at hand, and our impatience near the boil. One more thing. Other than that one time we haven't dealt with DHL since, but we have told the story a number of times. Moreover, DHL has never probed us to find out why our business with them has stopped.

POINT: *Courtesy can be contagious. Treat your customers as you would want to be treated—treat them even better than you expect to be treated—and they not only remain satisfied, they can become your most constant supporters and most effective spokesperson. Do otherwise, and they may go elsewhere for the products and services they require. Remember that you never know what a customer expects until you probe to find out.*

To Review

PROBE
YOUR CUSTOMERS
HAVE IDEAS

For whatever reason, people can appear to be unwilling to get involved. Nevertheless, these same people can have good ideas and can be quite vocal. Businesses interested in creating positive comments and avoiding negative ones should push their customers to reveal their feelings.

KEY POINTS

- *Form focus groups among your customers to find out what they think about and expect of your operation.*

- *Make sure customers are receiving the same high quality of service no matter when they come or call or whom they contact in your organization.*

- *Capture first impressions! They are generally more indicative of a person's true feelings and critical to getting the customer to come back.*

- *Get on the telephone, onto the sales floor, and out among your customers regularly to find out what customers feel and may say to others about your organization.*

- *Never be complacent. Remember that negative word of mouth commentary can start before you even realize that there is a problem.*

- *Asking for referrals from satisfied customers is another way of making word of mouth promotion work.*

- *If customers lose time because of your mistake, make sure they are well compensated for the inconvenience involved.*

- *Treat negative comments as an early warning system of a possible problem and turn them into an opportunity to improve.*

- *Treat customers even better than you would expect to be treated—and they will repay the kindness many fold in their conversations with friends, relatives, and associates.*

REWARD
YOUR CUSTOMERS
DESERVE RECOGNITION

WISH YOU WERE HERE

AN APPLE A DAY

I COULDA BEEN SOMEBODY

HOW CAN I BE OF SERVICE?

HERE, TAKE THIS

HAPPY BIRTHDAY TO YOU

WHAT'S IN A NAME?

THIS WEEK'S LOTTERY IS
EXPECTED TO BE WORTH...

MEMBERS ONLY

I CAN GET IT FOR YOU WHOLESALE

PASSPORTS FOR PATRONS

WON'T YOU HAVE A
PIECE OF CHOCOLATE?

REWARD
YOUR CUSTOMERS DESERVE RECOGNITION

> WISH YOU WERE HERE

Every business interested in word of mouth commentary ought to at least give postcards away to its customers.

It used to be that every hotel put postcards in its guest rooms hoping that customers would send one to a friend. It was an inexpensive way to do nationwide and international advertising. Then all of a sudden the cards became more of a rarity.

We think the decline began around the time that Howard Hughes took control of a major portion of the hotel business in Las Vegas. We were consulting for a Hughes company at the time. His people gave the impression that it was far better to *sell* something in the hotel gift shop for a profit than *give* it away for free in the rooms. Sound theory; lousy appreciation of the power of word of mouth commentary as a marketing medium.

The postcard is one of the most powerful instruments to stimulate conversations. Recipients generally thank the sender when next they talk, giving the sender an opening to tell his or her stories from the trip, describe in detail the places visited, and perhaps make a recommendation to the recipient that will increase your future business.

POINT: *The potential of a postcard to stimulate word of mouth commentary is so strong that every retail establishment not only ought to give cards away, but ought to* **pay** *for the stamps to mail them as well!*

REWARD
YOUR CUSTOMERS DESERVE RECOGNITION

AN APPLE A DAY

Giving away an apple leaves a good taste in the mouths of customers in more than one way.

The Stanford Park Hotel in Palo Alto, California, always has a large basket of fresh fruit on the reception desk, complimentary cookies in the lobby, and a generous range of national and local papers available in its restaurants. Others in the hospitality business similarly pamper their guests with impressive treats. Nearly everyone who travels appreciates the thoughtfulness behind these efforts.

These are the kind of *unusual* services that evoke an expansive comment when someone at home asks: "How was the trip?" or "Did you like the hotel?" Whenever a person can go beyond "Oh, fine," and launch into a description of something that stuck in his or her memory, word of mouth promotion has begun. Those who listen to the stories may not later remember the place, or the name of the hotel, or even the nature of the special service that triggered the discussion; but they will likely recall the *feeling* that the original comments conveyed. The next time these listeners are about to go to the same place, they may reinvestigate the details to try to duplicate the experience.

A complimentary cup of coffee is now so ubiquitous that it may no longer be "remarkable." For other businesses, we have in mind such off-the-wall (but tangentially related) giveaways as insurance agencies arranging to have annual fire extinguisher rechargings offered to clients or law firms organizing free quarterly safety inspections for their best clients.

POINT: *Remember that word of mouth comments only really begin with the unusual.*

I COULDA BEEN SOMEBODY

The desire for recognition is a powerful one in our society.

In a world that relies on numbers to distinguish one person from another—identification numbers, account numbers, membership numbers—finding a way to recognize *individuals* becomes increasingly important. It is a recognition that goes beyond calling a customer by name—although that, in itself, is very nice and the basis for continuing favorable word of mouth commentary. Giving a few good customers the means to provide something of value to *their* relatives, friends, or associates rewards that customer with a feeling of *power*. All of a sudden, the customer becomes someone to be recognized, someone of importance.

Do you know anyone who doesn't appreciate the chance to acquire some needed product through a wholesale source? Do you know anyone who is given a season ticket holder's seats for a concert or sporting event that doesn't feel special while being guided to the seat? Do you know anyone who refuses to ride in a first class seat on an airplane when the coach section has been oversold?

Marlon Brando's famous lament in the film *On The Waterfront*—"*I coulda been somebody*"—refers to having to throw a boxing match. Most people—when they think about society and their daily lives—might echo a similar lament:
>   "*I wanna be somebody.*"

POINT: *The concept of* **empowering** *someone is important in generating word of mouth comments and bringing in new business!*

REWARD
YOUR CUSTOMERS DESERVE RECOGNITION

HOW CAN I BE OF SERVICE?

These words when spoken by someone high enough in an organization to make decisions are nearly magical today.

All of us have known the frustration of standing in line or waiting on the phone to have simple questions answered or minor problems solved by a large bureaucratic organization. Some companies have attacked the problem with competent technicians available through 800 numbers. General Electric, for one, has something it calls an "Answer Center"—a 24-hour telephone service to resolve customer problems.

All large companies can use the same type of concept to stimulate favorable word of mouth comments by creating a *liaison office* for some of their customers. These customers would be informed of a special private telephone and/or FAX number—to use themselves *and* to give out to their relatives, friends, and associates—to reach a specific individual in that office. Whenever someone other than the customer contacted the office, the liaison person would ask how the caller was referred. If the caller had the name of someone *empowered* to offer the expediting service, they would hear the magical words: "And how can I be of service to *you*."

Expediting programs that exist in name only—really don't produce results for their callers, can't actually solve problems, never seem to do more than take information down—can be dangerous. Hopes raised and then dashed produce the fertile soil in which negative word of mouth commentary thrives.

POINT: *Expediting services that work should generate an enormous amount of favorable word of mouth comments. As a basic lesson, remember: do it right or don't bother doing it.*

REWARD
YOUR CUSTOMERS DESERVE RECOGNITION

See what happens when the customers of a business give away things of value rather than the business itself giving those same things away.

HERE, HAVE THIS

Whether your business has season tickets, a table at a charity event, or special offerings for selected customers, there is a world of difference between the manager of the business selecting the recipients of these privileged opportunities and a *favored customer* doing the selection. When a manager makes the choice, he may feel like a father indulging his kids; when the *customer* makes the selection, the customer may feel so good that he or she is inspired to do sufficient business to justify receiving the reward again.

Here's an example. The owner of "Junior's," a West Los Angeles delicatessen, glides through the restaurant from time to time to present an entire chocolate cake to a customer for the *customer* to share with his or her table companions. The presentation, excitement, and appreciation never fail to create a stir within the restaurant. In fact, the owner of this delicatessen told *The Wall St. Journal* that he always ends up *selling* more slices of the cake and more whole cakes to *other* customers as a result of the ceremony than he does by merely describing the item on his menu.* In short, *giving* things away for others to distribute can be profitable!

POINT: *We believe that giving valuable things away inspires a lasting obligation. But we have even stronger feelings that those obligations are broadened and reinforced when your customers do the giving on your behalf. For us, these acts become a natural and inevitable way to create word of mouth comments about your goods or services.*

REWARD
YOUR CUSTOMERS DESERVE RECOGNITION

HAPPY BIRTHDAY
TO YOU

Send personal cards to your favorite customers from time to time, but with a little gift as well.

Note the following progression of reactions to something received in the mail:

- If a business sends a customer a *birthday card*, that is very nice.

- If a business sends a customer a birthday card *along with* a small gift, that is very thoughtful.

- But if a business sends a customer a birthday card along with a small gift for the recipient *and* a gift voucher for the customer to give to a friend, relative, or associate, that is both very generous *and* smart.^

What to do in the way of a gift for customers—and for customers to give away in honor of their birthday?

- Optometrists could give away new eyeglass cases, perhaps personalized or in the customer's favorite color or sample clearning materials.

- Engineering firms could provide special rulers, do space measurements, or give special computer lessons.

- Manufacturers could test and calibrate measuring devices—everything from mail scales to the office clocks—for their suppliers and the suppliers' contacts.

- All firms could share their season tickets to concerts, sporting events, or civic activities.

We believe that if a business does something that many others do, it will be appreciated. But if a business does something unusual that by itself tends to generate a conversation and in addition brings in new customers, that's clever.

POINT: *When a business is able to develop a personal relationship with its customers—cemented and nurtured through such devices as special birthday gifts—the customer is much more likely to talk about that business than about the businesses with which the customer only has a more formal relationship.*

REWARD
YOUR CUSTOMERS DESERVE RECOGNITION

WHAT'S IN A NAME?

Elegant concepts— often at no cost— are sometimes the simplest to put into play.

Some consultants deserve recognition for the elegant solutions they have proposed to problems presented to them. To the consulting trade, an elegant solution is one that is functionally effective, operationally simple, and financially attractive. Take the consultant who was asked to devise a no-cost way of limiting parking on the main shopping street of a medium- sized town serving a surrounding rural community. The town wanted the available parking spaces to turn over rapidly, but it didn't want to have to bother the police, hire meter maids, or install parking meters. The consultant's solution? Require everyone parking on the main street to turn on the car's head- lights for the duration of the stop. Fear of a dead battery got people in and out of the shops quickly. It cost nothing, and it worked.

Businesses seeking word of mouth support can accomplish the same end with other elegant solutions. How about something as simple and as flattering as naming an item after a customer? Restaurants often create new dishes or sandwiches, but they name them in honor of some celebrity; universities and hospitals tend to name schools and wings after contributors. But any business can use the same idea. Name areas of your business or particular services in honor of your customers and/ or suppliers. It won't cost you anything and it causes conversation!

> POINT: *Naming things after people is flattering and worthy of comment. Giving customers reasons to talk about a business is what word of mouth is all about. Put another way, if you don't give them something to talk about, they probably won't!*

Giving your customers tickets entitling their friends to participate in special drawings is another form of empowerment.

THIS WEEK'S LOTTERY IS EXPECTED TO BE WORTH...

The power of lotteries to attract mounds of money in small denominations is legendary. Columbia University, to cite just one example, grew on the proceeds of special lotteries conducted to support its development.

All lottery players share the dream of becoming enormously rich on the strength of a tiny investment. It is the driving force behind all lotteries; a dream that makes an otherwise dreary life sustainable for many.

While private lotteries are illegal and advertised drawings are subject to special legal considerations, we know of no restrictions on an enterprise allowing specially designated customers to select a friend, relative, or associate to chose a surprise gift from a pile of packages in a store or office. Businesses could make the gift selection process a part of an annual celebration of its going into business. The nice part about this idea is that it has the virtue of being a little different. It attracts the attention of a broad range of people, but it involves a limited number of participants—heightening their chances of winning something of special value to them. Best of all, it requires recipients to visit the store or business in order to participate in the prize drawing.

POINT: *Holding a special drawing and letting your customers select someone to be eligible for the prize serves two purposes: it empowers your customers and it introduces you to new people.*

REWARD
YOUR CUSTOMERS DESERVE RECOGNITION

MEMBERS ONLY

Creating a special document for your best customers to give to their contacts makes the concept of empowerment tangible.

We were involved in a variation on this idea several years ago—both its success and the problem it created. A client of our consulting firm built a Kentucky Fried Chicken restaurant. Just before the restaurant's grand opening, the owner was sent a handful of cards that entitled holders to a 10-percent discount on any item on the store's menu. The owner was pleased, but uncertain what to do with them.

She asked us for suggestions. We compiled a list of the *employees* of both the legal and accounting firms with which she did business. We calculated that some employees might live close-by and others with limited income would be pleased with the savings potential of the discount cards. We also figured that in appreciation for her thoughtfulness these employees might treat her needs with special care in the future.

We had taken the concept of empowerment to the point of giving our client an advantage. It worked! Everyone was delighted: the store started drawing people that might not ever have visited it; the professional advisors were able to provide their employees with an unusual fringe benefit; and the owner of the property received increased attention to her needs.

But some good things don't last. A positive word of mouth program suddenly turned sour. We heard that after thirty days the managers of the restaurant began refusing to honor the discount cards. They claimed they were only intended to be good during the month of the grand opening and that they had been issued by the franchisor rather than the local store. Others heard that the "printer" had left off an expiration date. Rather than make a fuss over the small amounts involved, the card holders accepted the change. But we also know that they have stopped going out of their way to buy at this particular outlet. Just as significantly, they also stopped *talking* about the restaurant.

POINT: *Offer a discount card or accord other special privileges to your customers to give away to their contacts, but make sure that the savings are real, exclusive, lasting, and clearly explained.*

REWARD
YOUR CUSTOMERS DESERVE RECOGNITION

I CAN GET IT FOR
YOU WHOLESALE

There is a difference in perceptions of cost between the people standing behind a cash register and those standing in front of it.

Many people are amazed to learn that the flower business can involve a 400 percent markup; that products sold directly to consumers on television may cost only 10 percent of their selling price; and that jewelry items often carry a cost to price ratio of 1 to 3.

Look at the subject of jewelry. A nice single row of cultured pearls may have a retail price in a showcase of $895. You can be almost certain that those pearls cost the retailer less than $300. Thus, when they go on sale at a 30 percent discount, the jeweler is still *doubling* his cost. Even a half-price sale—an enormous opportunity for most retail customers to save a significant sum of money—doesn't mean the jeweler is giving his merchandise away. Half off still leaves him with a *profit* of 50 percent on the cost of the goods.

Another way to empower your best customers is to allow them to send their relatives, friends, and associates to you for a *special* discount or service not available to the general public.

POINT: *By empowering some of your customers to award others the opportunity to receive a special discount or service, the new customers to your store receive something of high value to them but which may end up costing you relatively little. More importantly, these new customers may ask to do the same thing for their friends, perhaps even creating a kind of word of mouth*

REWARD
YOUR CUSTOMERS DESERVE RECOGNITION

PASSPORTS FOR PATRONS

Provide your customers with a document that empowers their friends, relatives, or associates to receive special privileges from your business.

Because discounting has been debased by one day sales, opening hour sales, pre-Christmas sales, and the like, giving a *monetary* discount to special customers may no longer be powerful enough to generate positive word of mouth comments. Moreover, those who talk about a firm want to think that their friends will always get a good financial deal when doing business there.

As a result, small business owners and managers can create a special kind of document for their best customers to give to *their* friends, relatives, or associates to receive some special *privilege*:

- Documents issued by a restaurant might entitle holders to a complimentary bottle of wine, special appetizer, or dessert as the *guest* of the customer who received the document to give away.

- An insurance agency, law office, or accounting firm might issue cards for their best clients to pass on to others to entitle the holders to send a FAX, get a document notarized, have a reservation or appointment arranged, produce a photocopy, or make a delivery—all at no charge to the card holder.

- Doctors might encourage some of their patients to offer passess to others entitling the recipient to a free blood pressure reading, a free immunization before a trip, or even telephonic advice on the efficacy of over-the-counter medicines.

- Retailers could offer friends, relatives, and associates of their best customers such free services as alterations, exchanges, or fashion consulting.

Some entrepreneurs who have tried special privileges have also sometimes restricted them to specific days, times, or amounts. The fear is always that some customer will abuse the offer. But we believe that it may be far better for those firms seeking to generate positive word of mouth comments to err on the side of generosity and swallow the occasional problem, rather than lace a good program with complications and restrictions that only lawyers can devise and decipher.

Here's another way to look at the matter of potential abuse. Let's say you offer clients and their friends free FAX privileges, and then the son of the friend of a good client presents a 10-page Valentine message for transmittal to London This might seem excessive and abusive until you realize that the $15 involved probably couldn't buy two lines in the classified ads for one day!

> **POINT:** *The cost to benefit ratio of word of mouth promotion is very attractive. It may well be the least expensive media available for the most effective results possible. But it certainly isn't entirely free. But then again nothing really is, is it?*

*"Would you like to be **my** guest?"*

WON'T YOU HAVE A PIECE OF CHOCOLATE?

Offering a sample gets people to try new things and then perhaps talk about them.

See's Candies in California offers every customer a piece of their finest chocolates to sample on each visit. Although many protest that it will ruin their lunch (dinner) or that it is fattening or not a filling they like, almost no one seems to refuse the gesture. The chocolate at See's is not only a way of getting people to try different kinds of chocolates, but it is a way of showing special appreciation to the customers for the business they bring.^ It is also a sure way to get people to start talking. Ask anyone who has been to a See's Candies store what is the first thing that comes to mind about the operation and we'll bet they mention the samples everyone receives.

Any business should be thinking about the type of free samples *it* might provide—on its own or in conjunction with a supplier—as a way to try new products, draw old customers back, and to get customers talking. Restaurants can serve different nibble foods; mechanics can provide free window washing fluid or gasoline additives; fertilizer manufacturers can send fruits or vegetables grown with their products; hotels can offer special souvenirs. The possibilities seem endless. For example, we learned that Central Magazines and Books in Philadelphia gives posters to its best customers in appreciation of their business. The clever thing is that these posters are obtained by the bookstore for *free* from publishers at various book shows its managers attend.

POINT: *It doesn't take a lot to be generous; it doesn't take much to be creative in dealing with your customers; but it does take style to establish a reputation with old as well as new customers.*

To Review

REWARD
YOUR CUSTOMERS
DESERVE RECOGNITION

Word of mouth comments about a product, service, or facility need to be sparked by something unusual. Giving your best customers the right to give *their* friends, relatives, or associates special privileges sparks the discussions that bring in new customers and creates the loyalty that make old customers stick with you.

KEY POINTS

- *Give blank postcards away to stimulate comments between sender and recipient.*

- *Provide remarkable treats for your customers if you expect them to help generate additional business through their comments.*

- *Empower customers to make special services of yours available to their friends, relatives, and associates.*

- *Empowerment may come in the form of a private telephone line to get information, place orders, solve certain problems.*

- *Empowerment can also involve honoring customers in front of their relatives, friends, and associates.*

- *Empowerment can happen when a nice gesture is made unusual, such as sending customers gifts for themselves and someone else on their birthdays.*

- *Honor your customers by naming something after them.*

- *Empowerment can be giving customers the right to award someone a chance to receive a special prize.*

- *Remember that once a business empowers its customers, the business must be cautious about altering the program in the future.*

- *Special discounts can be highly significant when customers make them available to a friend, relative, or associate, but not necessarily costly to businesses honoring them.*

- *When discounts are not appropriate, let customers award special services that the business provides instead.*

- *Finally, empowerment—if it is to cause positive word of mouth comments— has to be given and treated with style!*

INFORM
YOUR CUSTOMERS ARE
PART OF YOUR BUSINESS

JUST A NOTE TO SAY THANKS

NANCY AND I WANT TO...

ANSWER THE MAIL!

STAY IN TOUCH...PLEASE

I OWN IT

DID YOU HEAR THE ONE?

CAN YOU RECOMMEND SOMETHING?

YOUR BEST IDEA HERE...
IN THE NEXT EDITION

JUST A NOTE
TO SAY THANKS

Prolong the memory of an event, product, or service with something that carries a little more impact than just a note.

All of us have received thank you notes—from brides for a wedding gift, from guests who enjoyed a dinner party, and from friends who received some memento. They are nice to get, and they are a confirmation that what was sent or done was in fact received and appreciated.

But businesses interested in generating word of mouth commentary have to go beyond a perfunctory, "Thank you for the order," a mechanical, "Look forward to serving you again in the near future," or a brush off, "Your suggestion is being studied." These businesses can communicate new information as well as *reward* their customers for previous business.

Some ideas to add to a future thank you note might include:

- "When we receive our next shipment, we would be delighted to write to you and a friend to see it privately and to give you both a special ☐ % discount on all of our products."

- "We have noted your individual needs (preferences, likes, dislikes) in a special confidential file in our computer as follows: ☐. Please let us know if we have missed any or when changes occur so that we can continue to serve you in an appropriate manner."

- "Your suggestion is most welcome and has been entered in our annual award program for customer assistance."

- "Please let us know the next time you or a friend want to shop with us (or will be in town) so that we can provide you and/or your friend with complimentary transportation."

POINT: Make all of your communications personal and timely. People tend to take better care of friends than strangers. If you take care of them, they will take care of you.

"And don't forget to offer them citizenship."

INFORM
YOUR CUSTOMERS ARE PART OF YOUR BUSINESS

NANCY AND I WANT TO...

*Build your customers'
trust in you.*

By common agreement, Ronald Reagan was brilliant when he was communicating his ideas to the American people. We believe that one reason for his success was his ability to bring people into his confidence. His beguiling phrase that "Nancy and I want to..." made people feel connected to him.

We can learn from Ronald Reagan's example. Bring people into your confidence—make them feel that they are your partners on the inside of your business—and they will come to trust you with some of their most precious assets: their relatives, friends, and associates. No one interested in using word of mouth to develop greater business could ask for more. As trust in Ronald Reagan translated into an enormous vote of confidence at election time, so building trust among your customers should gain their support in terms of greater sales.

We urge business people to find ways to get on an informal, open, and trustworthy basis with their best customers. Try an occasional private letter to special customers discussing why prices have risen, why greater profits are specifically needed, what frustrates you about your competitors, or any other matter of genuine concern. If not by private letter or a special newsletter, let your best customers know about special opportunities in a billing stuffer, by a personal card, or orally during their visits to your facilities. Make these efforts to gain trust *selective*, *occasional*, and *worthwhile*.

POINT: *Trust customers with crucial information, and they are likely to trust you with consistent purchases.*

INFORM
YOUR CUSTOMERS ARE PART OF YOUR BUSINESS

ANSWER THE MAIL

Acknowledging all communications—even if you can't answer their specifics—can extinguish some customer anger and frustration.

Too often, letters go unanswered or get delayed as the institution waits for the right person to sign a response. In the absence of an answer, people who got worked up enough to spend the time and energy required to communicate in writing with an institution get angrier and more frustrated. They tend to relieve that anger and frustration by describing their problem or suggestion to relatives, friends, and associates. It is the beginning of potentially damaging negative word of mouth commentary.

A simple response not only stops negative comments before they begin, but can reverse them when a company finds a nice way to resolve a problem—a coupon, a free sample, having a representative call, or so forth. While there are crackpots, malcontents, and lonely people who will never stop communicating and can never be fully satisfied, they tend to have little credibility. Once discovered and then ignored, they won't do damage. The mistake is to think that every complaint and problem may fit the crackpot profile or that any suggestion that didn't come from within an organization is suspect.

POINT: *It is safe to assume that anyone who takes the time to write a letter also has the energy and interest to be a supporter or detractor through word of mouth comments.*

INFORM
YOUR CUSTOMERS ARE PART OF YOUR BUSINESS

STAY IN TOUCH...PLEASE

Invest in your best customers by "reaching out" to them at every opportunity.

A few years ago, one of us was so taken by the quality of a new Nissan Maxima that he wrote to the company's U.S. office. He wanted the individual who had "signed" the final inspection certificate at the factory—and posted it on a rear window—to know that the end user had found everything in order.

A few weeks later he got a very nice letter of appreciation telling him that our letter would be translated into Japanese and sent to the inspector. Everyone was pleased. But that is all he ever heard from Nissan. In fact, in the five years since, no one from Nissan has been back in touch with him on *any* subject for any reason.

Given the cost of acquiring new customers through paid advertising or public relations efforts, it makes sense to keep what you have already gained.^ In this case, one of us was already a "sold" customer; he had in fact enlisted as a word of mouth spokesperson through this letter. Rather than run the risk of allowing someone else to lure him to a competitor's product or something to sour the positive attitude about the product, wouldn't a program to keep him talking make sense? To do this, what about private showings of new models, invitations to some function, a newsletter, or an amusing greeting card on the anniversary of the product purchase as noted from the warranty information.

POINT: *Find a way to "Stay in Touch" with your best customers to keep them talking about you.*

INFORM
YOUR CUSTOMERS ARE PART OF YOUR BUSINESS

I OWN IT

Pride of ownership is a powerful stimulus for word of mouth.

CalTrans—the California Department of Transportation—has a program that encourages non-profit groups and private businesses to "adopt" a highway. These organizations take care of a segment of California's freeways and interstate roads—asking their people to help in clearing away accumulated litter, tending to the vegetation, reporting on the need for repairs, contributing funds, and so on—in return for roadside recognition.

In New York City, some 17 murals have been put up for "adoption." There, groups and individuals are being solicited for funds to clean and repair deteriorating and vandalized murals. Besides a tax deduction, the contributors gain the satisfaction of preserving an element of the nation's artistic heritage. In other jurisdictions, schools are put up for "adoption" to provide needed financial and instructional help.^

Variations of the concept are being tried elsewhere. The Federal government, for example, is involved in an Adopt-a-Monument program as an alternate means of providing necessary maintenance funds. Businesses can consider the same concept of "sharing" ownership of their facilities or their corporate treasures with outsiders. Customers, for example, could be made curators of special merchandise displays, guardians of public areas, or guides for historically worthy sites controlled by the business.

> POINT: *Giving customers ownership or participation in an aspect of a business gives them a linkage to the business, pride in its progress, and a valid reason to talk about it to others.*

DID YOU HEAR THE ONE?

If not discounts or other special advantages, why not give customers jokes to tell?

Traffic school is one of the ways motorists in California can eliminate a ticket from their driving records. These private schools are required to teach a standard, often tedious curriculum. To offset this, some traffic schools hire budding comedians to spice up the material.

Traffic schools featuring humorous instructors are very popular.^ It suggests that even in the most mundane circumstances, we all enjoy laughing. Norman Cousins, in his book *Anatomy of an Illness*, demonstrated that laughter could be a positive force in recovering from serious illnesses. Stand-up comics have become an important source of programming on cable channels, just as night clubs devoted to humor have been increasing in numbers in metropolitan areas.^

All of this suggests that businesses should think of humor as a source for generating word of mouth commentary. A constant flow of easy to tell, current jokes as part of a firm's recorded telephone messages, on the back of a receipt, on the monthly billing envelopes, as an insert with a mailing, as a regular part of a newsletter, or in any other format could become very popular. Recipients inclined to sharing stories or gossiping will delight in retelling the jokes. Most of all, a good joke very often evokes a question on its origins.

> POINT: *A business could not hope for a more positive reaction to any word of mouth program than one that evokes the specific question: "Where did you hear that one?" It can get a conversation started in the best possible way for the sponsoring business.*

IINFORM
YOUR CUSTOMERS ARE PART OF YOUR BUSINESS

CAN YOU RECOMMEND SOMETHING?

Everyone appreciates a recommended solution, even if you can't otherwise help to solve a problem.

How many times have you asked for directions to a place or for a particular item only to learn that the person you are talking with doesn't know the answer or have what you are looking for. It happens all the time. Nordstrom, for one, has built a huge reputation for splendid service. Their well-compensated, commission-earning sales associates are reported to go to great lengths on behalf of customers to research answers to inquiries, deliver purchases, tend to repairs, and even buy items from competitors that Nordstrom itself doesn't carry.

Any business can build a reputation as helpful and generate favorable word of mouth commentary when employees are supplied with a handbook of commonly asked questions and the best answers to provide.

In terms of word of mouth promotion, we believe that it is far better to point a customer in the direction of a competitor or to try to determine a reliable answer to a question than it is to leave any inquiry with a curt "I don't know" or "We don't do that."

POINT: *Word of mouth commentary can sometimes be like chess. Winning efforts often come about through a long-term strategy of consistently helping people rather than through programs that pay off on each move made.*

INFORM
YOUR CUSTOMERS ARE PART OF YOUR BUSINESS

The authors want to hear how others have used word of mouth advertising to further their businesses.

YOUR BEST IDEA HERE...
IN THE NEXT EDITION

If a word of mouth program has worked in your business—or if you have had a particular experience as a consumer that sparked you into making either positive or negative word of mouth comments—the authors would like to evaluate it for the next edition of *Talk Is Cheap*. Please write to:

Talk Is Cheap
The Americas Group
9200 Sunset Blvd., Suite 404
Los Angeles, CA 90069

As a reward for your effort, we will send you *two* free copies of the next edition of *Talk Is Cheap*—one for you and one to give to a friend, relative, or associate. Better yet, if we use an idea or story in a subsequent edition, we'll talk about *you* to our readers by giving you credit.

POINT: *The authors of this book are not the only founts of wisdom concerning good ideas for word of mouth programs. Once entrepreneurs and managers begin to concentrate on what they can do within the context of their own firm's products, services,*

To Review

INFORM
YOUR CUSTOMERS ARE A PART
OF YOUR BUSINESS

Sustaining word of mouth commentary comes from bringing your best customers into your confidence through honest and thorough communication. In an age where all information is valuable, special information will be highly coveted.

KEY POINTS

- *Keep detailed records on your best customers and look for ways to use that information to keep those customers informed of your operation.*

- *Share inside information about your business, your industry, and your outlook on the future as honestly as possible with your best customers—not to give trade secrets away or to give aid and comfort to your competitors, but to demonstrate the level of trust that you put in your customers and the faith you have in their continuing support.*

- *Answer every inquiry promptly—even if the answer is only an acknowledgment that the inquiry was received.*

- *Use warranty cards, past orders, and every other means available to get in touch with your customers. Surprise them on occasion—wish them a happy Arbor Day or a thoughtful Flag Day by saying hello without soliciting an order or asking for a favor.*

- *Give customers "ownership" in a key aspect of your business.*

- *Give customers stories to repeat or jokes to tell to get others to start talking about your business.*

- *Make sure everyone in your organization can make open and honest recommendations in areas collateral to your business.*

SURPRISE
YOUR CUSTOMER TALK
ABOUT FRESH APPROACHES

**REAL MARKETERS
DO IT DIFFERENTLY**

**BANNED IN BOSTON CAN BE
A BOON IN BALTIMORE**

**WHAT'S A
CONVERSATION PIECE?**

**IT'S ONLY A
NUMBERS GAME**

When it isn't different, it isn't worth talking about. If it isn't worth talking about, word of mouth is stifled.

REAL MARKETERS
DO IT DIFFERENTLY

Whatever it is that you really believe sets your firm or product or service apart from all others in the marketplace, do this:

FIND IT!

POLISH IT!

and

SELL IT!

Just as fingerprints have been accepted as a unique attribute of each person, so *every* business can demonstrate a special quality.^ It could be its:

- Locations
- Hours
- Prices
- Special features
- Unusual services
- Distinctive skills
- Reliable employees

Remember that even those products or services that are specifically designed to emulate another more famous offering are generally differentiated by *pricing!* Whatever it is, don't hide it—tell people why you are different, but be sure to give it to them in *Reader's Digest* form.

> POINT: *People are busy; they have lots of things on their minds. If you can get people to understand why you are different from others purveying the same products or services, they will be able to describe what makes your company special to their friends, relatives, and associates.*

SURPRISE
YOUR CUSTOMERS TALK ABOUT FRESH APPROACHES

If you want to encourage word of mouth comments, don't be afraid to use ways that make your product or service controversial, newsworthy, or special.

BANNED IN BOSTON CAN BE A BOON IN BALTIMORE

Salman Rushdie's publisher sold a lot of books after the Ayatollah Ruhollah Khomeini ordered Rushdie's death for alleged blasphemous statements in *The Satanic Verses*. The Cincinnati Contemporary Arts Center had record crowds for an exhibition of Robert Mapplethorpe's photographs soon after the District Attorney arrested the Art Center's Director for violating Ohio laws on child pornography. Martin Scorcese's film, *The Last Temptation of Christ,* sold a lot of tickets to people who might not have bothered to see the movie except for the protests by Christian fundamentalist groups. *Two Live Crew* became a household name only after a record store owner sold one of their albums despite a Federal judge's determination that the lyrics were obscene.

The list of these types of incidences are nearly endless.^ Two things are clear about them. They are among the most effective generators of word of mouth commentary and they are nearly impossible to fake. While some notorious hoaxes have been perpetrated (the 1983 "discovery" of Hitler's diary comes to mind), the intense attention drawn to these controversies usually reveals the flaws before too much money changes hands.

Marketers should be looking for opportunities for their products or services to be used by celebrities, prominent people, or newsworthy institutions. In Hollywood, for example, there are product brokers who place items in films and on television shows to enhance their visibility and acceptance.

In other cases, we have heard that some enterprising people have delivered samples of their products to a local morning radio shows. On occasion they get lucky—the DJ has noted the gift and discussed the product on the air.

> **POINT:** *As a matter of course, all marketers should be looking for ways to attach their products or services to any fad, topic, or matter in the news or to bring it before the public.*

SURPRISE
YOUR CUSTOMERS TALK ABOUT FRESH APPROACHES

By definition, a conversation piece is anything that creates a conversation—and thus word of mouth commentary.

WHAT'S A CONVERSATION PIECE?

A Christmas card remains a Christmas card—like dozens of others received each year—until something about it causes people to notice. At the moment that people *remark* about it, the card becomes a conversation piece. The cause may be its design, its color, its styling, its wording, the identity of the sender. What distinguishes it is not important, it is the *difference* that counts.

Businesses cannot expect word of mouth to help sell products or services unless something associated with the product or service has a jump on everything else competing for attention and people's time.^

While an inexpensive Christmas Card today may cost $.35 and a handsome one may run as much as $1.35, it is our view that in the competition to create word of mouth commentary, it is far easier to create a conversation piece by buying the less expensive card and including a $1 bill for the recipient to give to his or her favorite Christmas charity than it is to buy the more expensive card.

POINT: *If you want whatever you do to promote your business to be* **talked** *about, just be sure to do it a little differently!*

SURPRISE
YOUR CUSTOMERS TALK ABOUT FRESH APPROACHES

IT'S ONLY A
NUMBERS GAME

*One comment
can reach many
people!*

While we have argued that word of mouth advertising has the kind of intense impact that gets people into the movies, keeps food products on supermarket shelves, and brings new patrons to professional offices, we have not talked in quantitative terms—terms often traditionally used in any discussion of advertising media or public relations campaigns.

We believe that every positive and negative comment generated has the potential to reach a lot of people. Forget colleagues and associates for the moment. Just look at the *family members* that could be involved:

Spouse
Children
In-laws
Parents
Uncle/Aunts
Cousins
Grandparents
Great grandparents

In today's extended families, there are an ever increasing number of linkages formed—parents get divorced and remarried (acquiring new relations in the process), kids get married and bring in new sets of in-laws to the family, and any number of uncles, aunts, cousins, and grandparents simply live longer.

The more surprising your effort to gain word of mouth commentary, the more first-wave conversations that will be repeated. These initial recipients of the information will be sufficiently impressed to repeat it to *their* contacts.

Count the number of friends, relatives, and work colleagues with whom you tend to chat about personal events and news items during a week. Each of these people will be talking to their extended family members and associates as well. While they might not repeat all the stories they hear to all of their friends, relatives, and work colleagues, any major positive or negative impression about a product or company or service might filter through to at least some of them. In short, the potential audience for any word of mouth comment can be perfectly enormous.

> **POINT:** *If a few people are sufficiently impressed by a firm's products, services, or activities, the number likely to hear about it can be mind boggling. Talk is not only cheap and effective, it can be very powerful as well.*

"Now in this scene, I want all of you to pass the word."

To Review

SURPRISE
YOUR CUSTOMERS TALK
ABOUT FRESH APPROACHES

Word of mouth comments are generated when observers find something *worthy* of comment. Simple as that! Of course, every observer has a slightly different threshold of what is considered worthy. Generally, though, something is worthy when it is different enough to cause surprise! But don't go too far with the concept of surprises. A doctor's patients, for example, would not appreciate any surprises and might talk negatively about the doctor if an aspect of a treatment turned out to be "surprising."

KEY POINTS

- *Find the comparative advantage of your product or service and make sure you exploit that advantage among your potential customers.*

- *Products or services that make news generate word of mouth commentary.*

- *Look for ways to elevate the usual or expected to the unusual and the unexpected.*

- *Get ready to handle the new customers you may see once you do something to surprise your customers!*

SAMPLE CASE STUDIES

Here are some examples of how several different types of businesses might employ word of mouth promotions to their advantage. Before deciding what might work in your situation, look at how your customers perceive you and at such local conditions and individual constraints as available capital, competitive forces, community expectations, timing details, and other like items. Once you have analyzed these aspects of the commercial environment, you can adopt an appropriate word of mouth strategy for your business.

A Barber Shop in a Rural Community

This is the type of sole proprietor business—compared to a chain of hair salons in a metropolitan area advertising on television—that can effectively use word of mouth promotions to add new patrons to its customer lists. A barber might present his current best customers with cards to give to out-of-town visitors or to the owner of a local diner to present to newcomers. The card should have the presenter's name written in and might entitle the holder to an introductory free shave, shampoo, facial treatment, manicure, shoe shine, and/or to receive a complimentary sample of a cologne, hair tonic, or other private label product. Note that the purpose, as always, is to create ways to *stimulate* word of mouth conversations. Since some customers might understandably be hesitant to initiate a conversation about their barber to an out-of-towner or some newcomer, make the task easier by arming the customer with things of value to give away. Finally, find ways (free haircuts, facials, shoulder massages) to continually reward your best customers for giving out the cards.

An Instant Printer in an Urban Area

Non-chain printers are usually reduced to sending mailers or distributing flyers when trying to attract new customers from businesses within a few miles' radius of their shop. But direct mail and hand delivered pieces are becoming increasingly expensive and enormously competitive. So we would recommend trying to stimulate a word of mouth promotion to see if that might also help a business grow. Printers might adapt our *Won't You Have a Piece of Chocolate?* concept by giving away specially imprinted scratch pads, daily planners ("Things to Do/Calls to Make"), calendars, or anything else a business may need in its everyday activities and that a printer can produce fairly cheaply. These or other items, given to a good customer to pass along to *their* customers, creates good will for with the original customer and provides an opportunity for them to recommend the printer to others.

A Spice Importer Selling to Food Processors

Firms that do not deal with the general public in the course of conducting their business can also benefit from word of mouth promotions among both their suppliers and their customers. Take the case of a firm that imports exotic leaves, seeds, and saps—the ingredients that give brand name products their distinctive flavors, appearances, and aromas. Such a firm might adapt the concept of *Get Me My Agent* by giving colleagues in foreign countries—their lawyers, accountants, freight forwarders, laboratory technicians, drivers, and others who assist in the conduct of the business abroad—a wide variety of useful ad specialty items to make available to new potential suppliers of the essential leaves, seeds, and saps. The importer can also make an impression by sponsoring an annual trip to some of the spice producing areas—trips for their customers and/or for their customers to give away. As to the purchasing agents who buy the exotic materials that the firm imports from abroad, we would suggest trying the *Nancy and I Want to...* approach. Recall that the idea is designed to pull customers into your confidence by talking about proprietary, sensitive, and little known information. Purchasing agents may have ethical problems accepting special gifts or anything with more than incidental monetary value, but they would likely have no hesitation in accepting useful information. Sharing such information with colleagues in non-competitive businesses could be the start of a word of mouth campaign that attracts new customers to the importing firm.

Specialty Retailer Selling to Ethnic Community

Some retailers, by virtue of the types of products they sell, their location, or the nature of their customer base, do very little promotion now. Kosher food markets, for example, tend to think that only price and/or product availability draw new customers in. They may be correct. But they may also be a little shortsighted. We would recommend looking at some word of mouth possibilities as a way of bringing outsiders to the store. We like anything that has to do with giving something to the children that visit the store with an adult—balloons, coloring books, pencils, sweets, dried fruit, and so on. (See *Kids Are People, Too*) This will get the kids talking to their friends as well as their parents about returning to the store and will keep the parents coming back as a way to give the children a free treat as well as an outing.

A Machine Tool Maker in an Industrial Area

Machine tool makers are the heart of any industrial economy. They build the devices that turn out the manufactured goods that others consume. For example, a manufacturer of an industrial lathe—a machine capable of shaping several pieces at the same time—would be a crucial supplier to a furniture manufacturer. Machine tool makers are strong candidates for several word of mouth promotional ideas. One of the most attractive is *Misery Loves Company*—our idea to ask a firm's best customers to act as "Adjunct Consultants" concerning its products. While trade journal advertising, a direct mail card deck, or some other means of promotion may bring an inquiry in the door, it won't close the sale. The sale of something as durable as a machine tool will, of course, depend on price and delivery schedules and the reputation of the manufacturer, but often it is a word of mouth testimonial that *clinches* the sale.

A Restaurant along a Lonely Highway

Traveling between Los Angeles and Laughlin, Nevada—a new gambling resort on the Colorado River—is not quite the same as traveling between Riyadh and the Kuwaiti border in Saudi Arabia. But it is bleak in its own way. What if you were a restaurant owner along the highway connecting the two cities. Are there word of mouth techniques that you could use to build your clientele? As strange as it may seem, we think so. We are particularly fond of the concept we call *The Pen is Mightier Than...*—the idea of having preimprinted postcards available for patrons. The restaurant's postcard might feature a picture of its exterior, a map to its location, and/or a copy of its menu. The identification caption on the back might hint at how far it is from certain landmarks ("halfway between...;" "a nice break on the way to...;"), any of its special features (changing rooms, pay showers, dog runs), the restaurant's special dishes, or even a discount of 10 percent or 15 percent off of any order placed by the recipient. Leave the cards on the tables with a little sign that the restaurant will pay the postage. The restaurant has not only laid the groundwork for some word of mouth promotion between the sender and the eventual recipient, but has also fixed the restaurant in the mind of the customer for a possible return visit.

Land Developer Dealing with a Government Agency

We think there is so much potential for stimulating word of mouth promotion that it can be used when no product, service, or activity is directly involved. Just as investment firms use tombstone ads in magazines and journals to keep their name before a specialty public, and just as businesses take ads in the programs produced for charitable events to enhance their reputation, so we see the possibility of using some of the word of mouth techniques we have discussed to generate good will. Take the case of a wholesale land developer who acquires the permits and does the grading before selling the lots to various home builders. While the development company can use word of mouth techniques to promote land sales to home builders, it can also use other such techniques to improve its dealings with government agencies. We have in mind here a number of the concepts that build a base for favorable word of mouth commentary among the officials that must approve any request or application. For example:

- *Doesn't Anybody Know?*—the concept of the institutional memory to compare the current request or application with other requests and applications of the past.

- *"Be All That You Can Be"—and Other Such Promises*—the concept that businesses who want to build a favorable word of mouth promotional program need to be honest with their audiences about all aspects of their business.

- *Stay in Touch...Please*—finding ways to keep the government informed of everything material to its consideration.

Finally, recall that we approach some word of mouth promotions like moves in a chess game. It isn't always the next move that counts, but one that will come later on. We view the use of word of mouth promotional activities among government agencies in the same light. It isn't that a word of mouth campaign will necessarily result in securing a permit or getting the approval sought right away, but it is that any word of mouth program can help achieve those results in the future.

Remember that whatever the business or its circumstances, word of mouth promotions can be designed and stimulated by imaginative business people who understand its effectiveness and appreciate its low cost.

CONCLUDING NOTES

As one business person has noted: "The remarks people make...to their friends are always of more value than the boasts [a business] makes about itself."* Given the recognition that word of mouth advertising has achieved among marketing specialists, it is perhaps surprising that relatively little has been written about the subject. Indeed, what has been published tends toward analysis—*why* word of mouth comments may be generated—rather than *how* to make word of mouth work for a particular business.^

For instance, one study suggests that word of mouth comments can both *inform* and *influence* others on products. In fact, those whose own behavior toward a particular product resulted from interpersonal communication are believed to be more likely to stimulate others to buy the same product. While knowing that fact makes interesting conversation at a marketing meeting, it may not be terribly helpful to a manager with a tight advertising budget looking for ways to stimulate word of mouth conversations about his or her product, service, or facility.

Perhaps the most important study on the subject was prepared by John Arndt, then an assistant professor of business at Columbia University, for the Advertising Research Foundation. His 1967 effort seems to be the most extensive single academic treatment of the subject, and his overall conclusion is telling:

> Word of mouth emerges as one of the most important, if not the most important, sources of information for the consumer...

Arndt also points out that:

> [While] mass media...dominate[s]...the [product] awareness stage [of advertising]...word of mouth is the most frequently used source [of information] at the [product] evaluation stage.*

In fact, Michael Ray of Stanford University believes that a good product, good service, and good communication are all necessary to develop what he calls "personal testimonials." In looking at how these personal testimonials may work, Arndt found that word of mouth creates two categories of conversationalists: the communicators and the receivers.

> [They are both]...active, independent participants in the mass communications process. Receivers often initiate product conversations by asking communicators for information. Communicators play an active role by filtering and interpreting mass media information [for receivers].*

Although measuring the effectiveness of word of mouth promotion has proven difficult for many marketing managers, some interesting studies have been conducted. Campbell Soup, for example, learned that 56 percent of the homemakers they recently surveyed had received two specific movie recommendations in the previous three months, while only 15 percent had heard good things about something like a spaghetti sauce. Yet, of those that did get a favorable recommendation on a sauce, an impressive 82 percent then followed up the discussion with a purchase of the item recommended.*

Numbers like these suggest that additional measurement may not always be necessary for some large businesses. It may simply be enough to assert that word of mouth *works*. It has also clearly worked when a brand name becomes the generic description for a product. In fact, in such cases it would seem that word of mouth has achieved all that it can possibly be expected to achieve.

While lawyers for such firms as Coca Cola and Xerox understandably work ceaselessly to protect the value of brand name identification their companies have been successful in establishing, the marketing personnel in the same company have to be pleased when the public starts to use their product's name as the descriptive term for a particular item. In some cases, brand names become so entrenched that many people are hard pressed to find a generic term to describe such proprietary products as :

Band Aid
Kleenex
Q-Tips
Thermos
Velcro

Xerox
Yo Yo
Zipper

How many people would routinely ask a hotel housekeeper to provide a fresh box of "facial tissues" or would walk into a dry cleaners to see if they could repair a broken metal fastener on a pair of pants? It would seem that when a product name becomes the *common name* for an item, its market share goes ballistic—an enviable position for any enterprise to achieve.^

A few product names, of course, entered popular usage without adequate protection for the developing company. As a result, the courts have in effect removed their right to capitalization as the name of something distinctive. Escalator and aspirin come to mind as prominent examples of brand names gone generic.

In other cases, brand names once used as generic descriptions of a particular function no longer seem to serve that purpose. These products eventually were overtaken by acceptance of competitive products or by the march of time. For example: Victrola used to describe *all* phonograph players, just as Frigidaire was the preferred term for any refrigerator. Other such brand names live on as generic terms, but not necessarily in the United States. In England, for example, "hoovering" is still an accepted verb for the act of vacuuming, and a ball point pen is still sometimes referred to as a "biro" (after the company that first mass marketed these writing instruments).

Word of mouth has also probably achieved all that it can when a product name establishes itself as a form of measurement. We have often heard people talk about the *Rolls Royce* of stapling guns or the *IBM* of machine tool manufacturers.^ Companies such as Federal Express and McDonald's, as well as Mercedes and Cadillac, are also measurement names. For these companies, the reference suggests that they are considered the epitome of product quality and service. No more other than their name need be said to convey everything that a word of mouth promotion wants to convey. Although a wonderful position to reach, it is not an easy one to maintain in the face of competitive forces seeking weak points and special niches to exploit in what, by definition, looks like a lucrative business.

Other than generic names and forms of measurement, word of mouth has also clearly worked for a company when its product or service is identified in the public's mind with a particular function or property.

Look at these companies:

Kelley's Blue Book
This authoritative pricing guide for used automobiles serves as the basis for nearly every public and private activity concerned with car valuations.

Thomas Guides
The maps produced by these private map makers serve as universal descriptions of areas, streets, and communities in the places where they are published.

Hansard's
Just as the Congressional Record contains the official proceedings of the U.S. Congress, so Hansard's is the equivalent name for the proceedings of the British House of Commons. Few realize, however, that it is also the name of the private firm that compiles these verbatim reports.

Rice-a-Roni
This Quaker Oats Company brand is umbilically tied by its advertising slogan to the singsong phrase—"The San Francisco Treat."

Burma Shave
This cosmetic product provided roadside poems for generations of automobile travelers and as a result maintained high name recognition. (If You Don't Know/Whose Signs These Are/You Can't Have Driven/Very Far/ Burma Shave).^

Not every business executive, of course, can hope to have his or her new product or service identified in the public's mind by a brand name. That takes good fortune, time, and consistency to achieve. But trying to get a product or service firmly established in the marketplace ought to lead every business executive to explore how word of mouth promotions can be of use.

SPECIAL OFFER

If you think that a friend, relative, or associate might benefit from some of the ideas or discussion in *TALK IS CHEAP*, we invite you to fill out the Certificate below and send it to that individual for completion of the reverse and submission to the publisher. Please follow these simple steps:

- Be sure to provide the individual's name you recommend for a copy of *TALK IS CHEAP* in the box.
- Be sure to provide your own name, address, and the date that you mailed the certificate in the space at the bottom.

The individual you recommend will acquire a copy of the book directly from the publisher at a cost well below its retail price.

While your only reward at this time for making this recommendation is the pleasure of doing someone else a favor, be assured that the authors intend to create a periodic newsletter covering other ideas and examples of how to stimulate word of mouth advertising. Individuals whose names appear on a certificate will receive a *free* subscription to the Newsletter and will also be eligible to purchase any subsequent editions of *TALK IS CHEAP* at a substantial discount.

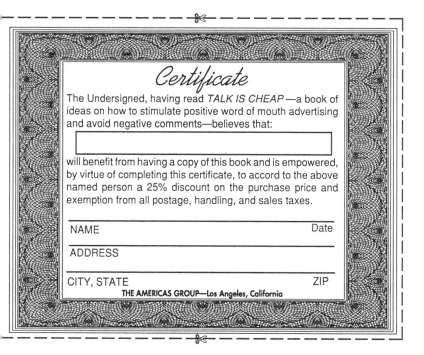

Certificate

The Undersigned, having read *TALK IS CHEAP*—a book of ideas on how to stimulate positive word of mouth advertising and avoid negative comments—believes that:

will benefit from having a copy of this book and is empowered, by virtue of completing this certificate, to accord to the above named person a 25% discount on the purchase price and exemption from all postage, handling, and sales taxes.

NAME   Date

ADDRESS

CITY, STATE   ZIP

THE AMERICAS GROUP—Los Angeles, California

When you have completed the certificate on the reverse, cut out and present to a friend, colleague, or associate for completion of the information below.

THE AMERICAS GROUP
9200 Sunset Blvd., Suite 404
Los Angeles, California 90069

Please send one copy of *TALK IS CHEAP* at the special reader's price of $7.46 ($9.95 cover price less 25% special discount and exemption from postage, handling, and sales taxes) to:

NAME

☐ Check/Money Order Enclosed

COMPANY

MAILING ADDRESS

☐ Charge My VISA/MC Account

CITY, STATE AND ZIP

Account Number   Name on Account   Exp. Date

( )

Signature   Telephone Number

ALPHABETICAL LIST OF
IDEAS AND THOUGHTS

ABOUT THIS BOOK
AND ITS AUTHORS

The idea for this book began to take shape as a result of a conversation between father and son one day last year. We were ruminating over the fact that of *all* forms of promotion available to the travel and tourism industry, word of mouth advertising seemed the most important source of new and continuing business. Yet it was something that travel and tourism companies did little to stimulate while they spent large sums on other, sometimes less effective, forms of promotion.^ Before describing that conversation further, a little background on the father and son might prove helpful:

Godfrey Harris, the father, has been a public policy consultant based in Los Angeles, California, for the past 24 years. He began consulting after brief careers as a university lecturer, an intelligence officer in the U.S. Army, a foreign service officer with the State Department in Washington, DC, and a management analyst in the Office of Management and Budget. As President of Harris/Ragan Management Group, he has focused his consulting activities on tourism development and commemorative events. He holds degrees from Stanford University and the University of California, Los Angeles.

Gregrey J Harris, the son, specializes in direct marketing. He began his business career operating his own photography business dedicated to legal subjects and managing major accounts for Harris/Ragan. Later, he conducted market research and developed a data base for cable television' s Financial News Network. Since 1988, he has managed direct marketing projects for Hewlett-Packard. He holds a BA in economics from the University of California, Santa Barbara, and an MBA in both marketing and finance from the University of Southern California.

Our discussion about word of mouth advertising in the travel and tourism industry concluded with the thought that *most* people rely on others for information about a place to go or a new site to see before committing to spend the time or money involved in a visit. We were sufficiently intrigued by the implications of the hypothesis to look for corroboration in the formal literature on advertising. We found almost nothing. When we began to talk to colleagues and contacts about the subject of word of mouth advertising, we learned that, while it is accepted by most people as an important factor in the success of any business, it is not something that they think can be readily measured or easily managed.

As we pursued the subject further, we came to accept the point about measurement. But we didn' t necessarily agree with the idea that word of mouth advertising couldn't be *managed* like any other form of promotion. So we started formulating ways that word of mouth *might* be controlled by business people. As we traded our string of ideas back and forth, it dawned on us that with a little common sense and a lot of imagination, word of mouth promotions could probably be successfully influenced. Godfrey Harris began testing the theories with clients. After a while, the examples and the experiences became the basis for this book.

In setting our ideas down, our goal has been a simple and practical one:

> *To give business people effective ways to stimulate and sustain positive comments about their products or services and suggest techniques to contain negative comments before they do damage.*

We hope that if we have done nothing else, we have demonstrated what we pointed out at the outset of the book: that positive word of mouth commentary does not have to be left to luck, and negative comments should never be left to fester.

We hope one more thing. That merchants, managers, and entrepreneurs who read this book will eventually teach us more about word of mouth advertising than we could ever learn by giving it detailed study and by reviewing what has been written on the topic. We have made a start; it is for others to refine it.

In compiling any book, the authors soon learn that they are responsible for all of its errors and will be forever indebted to others for most of its benefits. It is the case with this effort. In particular we very much appreciate the help we received from the following individuals:

- **Nancy Boss Art** for doing her usual outstanding job of clarifying our words, cleaning up our grammar, and vastly improving our thinking.
- **William P. Butler**, who read the book and then helped with the exacting job of captioning the cover cartoon.
- **Michael Gee** for helping with some of the brand names that have become generic names in England.
- **Michael DeKovner** who challenged some of our ideas and in the process sharpened our approach.
- **Barbara DeKovner-Mayer Harris** and **Eve Dutton Harris**, our wives, for suffering our preoccupation with this project as it developed over the last year.
- **Greg Mayer** for conducting some of the initial library research for the project.
- **Jamie Pfeiffer** for providing the original art work and design for the cover of the book.
- **John Powers** for his always appreciated advice on book design and typography.
- **James F. Ragan, Jr.**, an old friend and colleague, whose marvelous sense of humor is responsible for selecting the cartoons and creating the original captions used throughout the book.

We also asked people who are very special to us to read the book early in the process and give us their views on its approach.

- **David Harris** and **Michael Harris** in Los Angeles.
- **Ken Harris** in Santa Monica and **Mark Harris** in San Diego.
- **Alan Lister** and **Kenneth Katz** in London.

In addition, we received detailed comments from the following:

- **Rebecca Green, Michelle Hamond,** and **Tammy Traversino,** who carefully reviewed the book from their positions as business and marketing professionals.
- **Lucy and Jack Ballard**, small business owners, who read the manuscript from a potential user's viewpoint.

Godfrey Harris
Los Angeles, CA
Gregrey J Harris
San Carlos, CA

August 1991

BIBLIOGRAPHICAL NOTES

8   The importance of word of mouth commentary goes beyond the promotion of specific products, services, or activities. Languages, for example, change primarily as a result of word of mouth usage. The term "writer's block," in fact, was coined in 1947 by Dr. Edmund Beigler, a psychoanalyst, and came into the language through word of mouth acceptance of the concept. See Zachary Leader, *Writer's Block*, The Johns Hopkins University Press, 1990.

9   Opening night exit polls for the 1990 film *Home Alone*—a small budget picture that had a huge box office success—indicated that some 5 percent of the audience were seeing the film for the *second* time. Clearly, those who had been to the sneak preview had returned with friends. It was an indication of the importance of word of mouth advertising to films. (See *The Wall St. Journal*, December 4, 1990.) Movie companies aren't the only businesses to try to replicate a conversation in paid advertising. Take this one from Honeybaked Ham, Inc., under the heading: "What Nancy Foster's Guests Said About The Ham She Served."
     "She had this beautiful ham on the table...[pre-]cooked...and pre-sliced."
     "I hate her. Besides, she's got fat ankles."
     "She told me it had been baked and smoked...for almost 30 hours."
     "The woman's incredible."
     "I still hate her."

10   Food company data from Rick Dellacquilla, "Building Word-of-Mouth," *The Marketer*, November 1990.

     Information on security companies and their reliance on word of mouth commentary was found in "Public Relations by the Numbers," *American Demographics*, January 1991.

     Perhaps the most dismaying form of negative word of mouth commentary affected consumer product giant Procter & Gamble Co. Some people claimed that P & G's century-old corporate symbol of the moon and stars was evidence that Satan controlled the company. Rather than scoff at the ensuing whispering campaign, P & G successfully sued one couple for spreading the rumor. It is also reported to have answered more than 150,000 calls and letters about satanic rumors over the past 10 years. If nothing else, Procter & Gamble demonstrated how seriously it takes word of mouth comments. By the same token, P & G has recently decided to use another logo in certain commercial circumstances.

     The estimate of the impact of word of mouth comments on the theme park business was made to Kenneth Katz by Andy Grant of Grant Associates in London in October 1990.

13   We believe strongly that the more you exceed customer expectations, the more likely the customer is to *talk* about your business. But businesses need to understand the individual and aggregate *expectations* of both their existing and their potential customer base. Think about the companies with which you do business. Why do you tend to go to the same gas station, hardware store, or supermarket? Is it because of price? Is it a function of service? Is it because of location? In all likelihood, it is a combination of these factors. Collectively, they are called *value*. Value arises when benefits exceed costs. Thus:

$$Value = Benefits - Costs$$

Benefits include such obvious elements as product selection, credit terms, service levels, etc. The cost is both the price paid plus other things associated with conducting the transaction (your time probably being the major component). Put simply, customers who tend to receive higher values are happy customers. But receiving high value alone doesn't insure that a business will keep the customer or that the customer will recommend a business to others. Every customer has a set of unique *expectations* about how much value he or she anticipates receiving from a business. We state it this way:

Expected Value = Expected Benefits - Expected Costs

Consider these examples:

- Your semi-annual trip to the dentist typically produces sore gums, a thorough cleaning, and a hefty bill. The *value* derived is hard to measure. Most view these visits as producing benefits equal to or more than the cost of the visit. Since our expectations are fairly low, we continue to go year after year. *We argue that in industries where expectations of value are low, the potential to stimulate word of mouth promotions through surprising and imaginative programs is high.*

- The weekly trip to the cleaners is a little different. For many, it is accomplished on the way to or from work or as part of a round of weekend chores. Everyone tends to be in a rush to get in and out. Thus, the costs associated with these visits, independent of the cash outlay, are high. As a result, cleaners have a difficult time providing high *value* to customers because their expectations are high. *We argue that in businesses where customer expectations of value are high, the potential for negative word of mouth comments is greatest.*

To give customers higher value than they expect—thus increasing the potential for positive word of mouth promotion and reducing the threat of negative word of mouth discussion—adopt techniques in this book that increase customer benefits while reducing customer costs.

15 Ed Sullivan's New York *Daily News* column was entitled "The Talk of the Town."

19 American Telephone and Telegraph Company reports that 95 percent of customers who have a problem will do business with a firm again *if* the complaint is resolved immediately. See AT&T, *Fast Fact No. 3*, June 1991.

20 *The Los Angeles Times* has created a "Customer Satisfaction Center" to handle complaints. While the name sounds like it was created by a committee of government public relations specialists, it would seem to be on the right track if it can deal with praise as effectively as problems.

American Airlines is reported to be trying a new approach for handling customer comments. They have erected an interactive video booth, similar to an instant photo booth, in a few airport terminals. Passengers are urged to record their comments about a flight on tape immediately after landing. If nothing else, the *novelty* of the medium can be a stimulus for commenting. See *Advertising Age*, January 1991.

According to Jerry Plymire of Synergistic Systems of San Francisco, employees rarely encourage complaints because they hear them as *personal attacks* rather than as institutional feedback. But if it doesn't hear customer complaints, the business can't improve and may, in fact, generate negative word of mouth. See "What We Need is More Complaints," *Business Marketing*, March 1990.

22 As Frederick F. Reichheld and W. Earl Sasser, Jr., point out, loyal customers not only "do a lot of talking over the years and drum up a lot of business," but they are also increasingly profitable. While obtaining a customer may involve the cost of estimating,

advertising, promotions, credit checks, computer registration, and the like—some $51 on average for a new credit card account—statistical evidence demonstrates that as customers come to trust the new business and its procedures, they tend to do more and more transactions with it. Reichheld and Sasser writing in the *Harvard Business Review* ("Zero Defections: Quality Comes to Service," September-October 1990) also make a telling point when they say that keeping a customer loyal should be treated by accountants not as a cost, but as an investment.

24   Los Angeles City Councilwoman Joy Picus, conscious that city workers are often viewed as rude and inept, has focused attention on the problem of how to get civil servants to serve people rather than move paper. Picus took testimony at hearings from management specialists who asserted that a friendly smile or a cheery telephone greeting is not a substitute for substantive assistance. (*The Los Angeles Times*, February 26, 1991.) They clearly aren't, but they're not mutually exclusive either.

25   If you think about it, most advertising aimed at kids is designed to generate word of mouth comments, since the kids themselves don't have much discretionary income, and the products they want must be purchased for them. The amounts aren't small. *Time Magazine* estimates that some $850 billion spent per year in the United States is influenced by kids and refers to a 1989 Roper Report study that found that kids decide 74 percent of the time what leisure activities their families will pursue. (January 7, 1991). Hence, if you want to see some current efforts to stimulate talk about a product, sit down with your kids or grandchildren next Saturday and watch a few cartoon shows. It may prove to be the best few hours you ever spent—in more ways than one.

26   The City of Santa Clarita, California, recently took eavesdropping a step further. The Mayor of this Los Angeles suburb invited 50 local hairdressers, manicurists, and makeup specialists to a City Hall meeting. "Everyone talks to...beauty professionals. [So] we'd just like to know...[what] people are saying." Quoted in "Tidbits & Outrages," *The Washington Monthly*, July/August 1991.

MBNA of America is a credit card company based in Delaware. To cure persistent customer complaints and to reduce customer defections, senior executives spend four hours a month monitoring customer telephone calls from a special "listening room." This form of eavesdropping is practiced at other companies as well. See Frederick F. Reichheld and W. Earl Sasser, Jr., "Zero Defections: Quality Comes to Service," *Harvard Business Review*, September-October 1990.

30   The active use of word of mouth techniques by the owner of The Female Connection is not surprising; she is Barbara DeKovner-Mayer Harris, the wife of Godfrey Harris.

32   "Apologies have...," *The Wall St. Journal*, November 29, 1990.

Bill Johnson, program director for executive education at USC's business school, goes further by noting that faults must be corrected with "a gesture of penitence." *The Los Angeles Times*, May 1, 1991.

33   Colonel John Myers, director of advertising and public affairs for the Army Recruiting Command, seems to have considered the Gulf War an annoyance. He was quoted as saying: "We don't want to be misleading, but too much combat footage interferes with the long-term attributes of Army service that we want to portray: money for college, skills training, and relevance to a civilian career." Quoted in "Tilting at Windmills," *The Washington Monthly*, May 1991. Colonel Myers's views notwithstanding, post-Gulf War Army ads shown during the 1991 NBA finals stressed pride and patriotism as a reason for military service.

Despite the imaginative definitions created from military initials, the Pentagon continues to stick with its formal designations. Take MREs—Meals Ready to Eat. Robert Woodward, in his book, *The Commanders* (Simon & Schuster, 1991), notes that the field ration was referred to in the Gulf as Meals Rejected by Ethiopians—testimony to the geo-political sophistication of today's soldiers, who were seemingly aware of the depths of the famine in Ethiopia when they coined the phrase.

If the Army is reluctant to mention war as a possible consequence of military service, so cruise lines almost never talk about the possibility of experiencing bad weather while at sea. It is important to remember that just as exceeding *expectations* can generate positive word of mouth comments, so major *disappointments* can stimulate negative word of mouth comments. Forewarning of customers of possibilities may alleviate many future complaints.

"[images are like] mixing..." Quoted by Maureen Dowd in "Quayle Still a Bit Player," *The New York Times*, March 4, 1991.

37   Jerry Plymire, a San Francisco management consultant, points out that there may be another reason that businesses don't get complete answers: the questions may be wrong. He says that anyone seeking to learn about a business from customer reactions needs to learn how to invite *opinions* rather than merely elicit a *response*. Instead of "How is everything?" Plymire rephrases the question as: "What could we do better?" See "What We Need Is More Complaints," *Business Marketing*, March 1990.

43   It is not only travel agents who fail to see the world as their clients experience it. All businesses with voice mail and automatic phone systems may be in the same danger. People who know an extension can get through the phone system's verbal menus to reach the party wanted; those who don't have an exasperating time trying to remember the choices presented and reacting in a timely fashion. The point again is that all business people need to recreate themselves from time to time as their own customers to try to see how the public sees them.

49   The customer survey reproduced to the right comes from the Harris Ranch (no relation to the authors) in Coalinga, California. Take a moment to look at the questions. What does it mean, for example, if an anonymous person says that the Housekeeping Service is "fair"? Without a comparison to another hotel's housekeeping service or an appreciation of the customer's expectations, it can't mean very much. Moreover, how does it help a hotel to improve its service if another unknown person checks "excellent" in the overall rating? If that person enjoys economy hotels in major urban areas, the Harris Ranch may seem like the QE II ocean liner; but if a person is a frequent guest at Embassy Suites in resort areas, the Harris Ranch facility may only seem average. A simple addition to these kinds of surveys might be to ask about the last hotel a person stayed at, when, and whether for business or pleasure, in order to help determine a respondent's *expectations*. Finally, despite the protestations on the form in *italics* that comments *do* make a difference, we continue to have our doubts.

51   Director Mike Nichols expressed the need for freshness to an actor in this very memorable way: "Listen, what do you think your job is? To learn the words? The usher can do that. Your job is to say them for *the first time each time*." *The New York Times*, May 14, 1991.

53   If a FAX in every hotel room (now available at the new luxury Peninsula Hotel in Beverly Hills) may soon be common, others have talked about the fact that new *horizontal* transportation systems are necessary for shopping centers, resort complexes, theme parks, airports, convention centers and the like as the population ages. While the world has enjoyed vertical mass transportation systems for years in the form of elevators and escalators, relatively little has been done to make *horizontal* distances manageable.

   J. D. Powers & Associates is a market research firm specializing in customer satisfaction surveying. Long associated with ranking automobiles, it has recently begun to assess customer satisfaction in the computer industry. Conscious that satisfaction is a function of *expectations*, the Powers firm finds that people are delighted with their purchase when products tend to exceed expectations and are disappointed when products fail to meet those same standards.

55   Restaurants can benefit in another way from the principal of the Zagat survey. If a restaurant were to track reservation details on a personal computer—name, number in party, day of the week of the reservation, time of reservation preferred, etc.—some fairly useful analysis would soon be possible. Those who stopped coming or who changed the frequency of their visits might be contacted by phone, letter, or even a personal visit. In many cases, people's circumstances will have altered. But in others, these exchanges might indicate a problem that could be fixed. The caring demonstrated by the follow-up, along with some added incentive like a bottle of wine with dinner to entice the customer back, could themselves generate conversation if not increased business. For more information on the Zagat Surveys and their various editions, write to Zagat Surveys, 4 Columbus Circle, New York, NY 10019.

56   Studies conducted by Technical Assistance Research Programs in Washington, DC, find that only 4 percent of dissatisfied customers provide feedback to a *business* on what bothers them, but some 80 percent tell *others* about their problems. Not only is word of *dissatisfaction* spread rapidly, but some 91 percent never do business with that firm again. The reasons are interesting. Americans, it is believed, don't share their feelings easily; as a result, they tend to keep their unhappiness to themselves and vote with their feet by staying away from the firm afterwards. (See "What We Need is More Complaints," *Business Marketing*, March 1990.)

57   For a related thought, see the footnote for p. 37 above.

59   According to Frederick F. Reichheld and W. Earl Sasser, Jr., "One of the leading home builders in the United States...has found that more than 60% of its sales are the result of referrals." "Zero Defections: Quality Comes to Service," *Harvard Business Review*, September-October 1990.

62   One San Francisco consultant specializing in service notes that "complaints are...like mistakes. They are not good or bad, right or wrong. They are just *other ways of doing things*. " As such, complaints are opportunities to serve customers in different ways. See "What We Need Is More Complaints," *Business Marketing*, March 1990.

71   "Junior's... " *The Wall St. Journal*, November 21, 1990.

72   *Business Marketing* for February 1990 reported on an Arizona State University study of

gift giving. Some customers of an international industrial marketing firm were given a $10 leather business card file while a control group was given nothing. Then both groups were surveyed: "Those who received the gifts gave significantly higher ratings to the company's prices, quality, customer service, and delivery [and] were significantly more likely to contact the company on their next purchase."

81 See's Candies not only rewards its customers, it is famous for *listening* to them as well. In 1987, for example, the company decided to eliminate 14 varieties of candy from its inventory. A flood of angry letters followed. The company reinstated the two types that generated the most comments. More importantly, the company president sent a letter of apology to each customer who had written in as well as a gift certificate. Reported in *The Los Angeles Times*, May 10, 1991.

89 See footnote above for p. 22 for an example of the cost of customer acquisition.

90 The Santa Monica Alternative School, of which co-author Gregrey J Harris is a proud alumni, has recently been adopted by National Medical Enterprises, a major health care supplier, "to assist...in providing quality education."

91 Clements Communications of Concordville, Pennsylvania, recommends humor to motivate employees. They sell cartoon posters featuring "Herman." In one, a skier is buried face first deep in the snow with only the rear tips of his skis and the baskets of his poles visible. Herman, acting as a ski instructor, asks in the cartoon's caption: "Class...name four things he did wrong." The legend on the poster itself reads: "Reviewing mistakes is good. Avoiding them is better."

Among California's 450 traffic schools annually serving some 1.2 million errant drivers are such firms as World Famous Improvisation Traffic School and Lettuce Amuse U Comedy Schools. See *The Los Angeles Times*, June 26, 1991.

97 Even when commodity traders are dealing in a generic product on commodity exchanges, they are still differentiating themselves by *selling* their particular services in dealing with that commodity—clarity and speed of order execution, research, confirmations, etc.

99 Stories on products can impact a whole industry. Source Perrier's accidental contamination of its bottled water in 1990 caused the entire industry to be reviewed for its purity claims. On the other hand, Johnson & Johnson eventually boosted confidence in the over-the-counter medicine market by changing the packaging of its Tylenol products in response to the deaths of seven people from cyanide poisoning. See *The Wall St. Journal*, September 12, 1990.

101 A conversation piece is anything that makes an impression strong enough to cause a comment. It happened to us at an outlet center in Northern California. The center had an entire room set aside as a rest station for shoppers. It was a quiet place to just sit in a comfortable chair, relax, talk, and review purchases. No charge made, no food sold, no pressure placed on visitors to move along. All of that made it very *remarkable*—and we told others about how much we liked it.

111 "The remarks..." *Advertising in Modern Retailing*, Harper & Bros., 1954.

Among the formal studies we reviewed are the following: David A. Aaker and John G. Myers, *Advertisement Management*, Prentice Hall, Inc., 1982; Charles Ramond, *Advertising Research: The State of the Art*, Association of National Advertisers, 1976; Roger Barton, *Advertising Handbook*, Prentice-Hall, Inc., 1950; Michael L. Ray, *Advertising and*

Communication Management, Prentice-Hall, Inc., 1982; Jerry R. Wilson, Word of Mouth Marketing, J.W. Wiley and Sons, 1991.

Determining **how much** a business can afford to invest in word of mouth promotions is a function of the estimated *added* sales to be stimulated by your customers. In other words, if you assume that one out of 10, 25, or 50 customers will generate a new customer—and that the new customers will spend about what your current customers now do for items with a standard profit margin—then you have a basis for creating a word of mouth budget. Here is an example:

You run a small flower shop. You typically see about 80 customers a day, stay open 6 days a week, and operate 50 weeks during the year. Amazing as it sounds, about 24,000 customers come in each year. But the average individual customer stops by only every other month or six times a year. Because of this frequency factor, we assume you have a base of 4000 customers. The average purchase size is about $20. After covering your variable expenses, you enjoy a profit margin of 25 percent— or roughly $5 on each transaction. Here are two formulae which will help you estimate how much you can afford to spend on word of mouth advertising:

(Customer Base) x (Hit Rate) = New Customers

(New Customers) x (Number of Annual Purchases) x (Average Order Size) x (Average Profit Margin) = Incremental Word of Mouth Contribution.

If 1 percent of the base of 4000 customers stimulate a friend, relative, or associate to do business with you, you would have 40 new customers generated from word of mouth promotions. These 40 new customers—assuming they are satisfied—can be expected to shop 6 times during the year and generate $5 in profit each time they walk through the door. Thus, in the first year, your word of mouth efforts can generate an incremental $1,200 in profit.

So how much should you spend on promoting this program? All or most of it! You should be willing to spend what amounts to $.30 per customer during the year on any of the ideas we have described. But why spend all of your profit? Well, customers typically don't go away after only a year. In addition, they are more likely to refer someone themselves. On the other hand, what if $1,200 is not enough to create the kind of program you want? If you increase your hit rate to two percent—because of the novelty of your program—you could get 80 new customers and increase your profit to $2,500.

Finally, as you gain experience with word of mouth promotions, you might want to survey your new customers to determine exactly how many customers were generated with word of mouth advertising. As time goes by, you will develop a body of data that will allow you to refine your promotional budget on the basis of a precise cost/benefit ratio.

"Word of mouth emerges..." and "[while] mass..." Johan Arndt, Word of Mouth Advertising, Advertising Research Foundation, Inc. (New York), 1967.

112   "[They are both]..." Arndt, ibid.

Campbell Soup data taken from "Building Word of Mouth," The Marketer, November 1990.

113   A restaurateur notes that Perrier became the generic name for bottled water when it was the first, only, or obvious choice for customers. As he said, it was "second nature— like [asking] for a Kleenex" to request it by name before it was withdrawn from the

market in 1990. Now it has lost its special caché. *The Wall St. Journal*, September 12, 1990.

Rolls Royce set out to be the standard of an industry nearly from the start. In 1907, just three years after the company was formed, Henry Royce and Charles Rolls decided to prepare a car that would "cast a permanent image." They built the Silver Ghost and it is still on the road today. To sell the car, the company specifically "[pointed] out its advantages over the inferior products of that day." In other words, the company made, promoted, and demonstrated a car that was "remarkable." See *The Los Angeles Times*, December 30, 1990.

114   The quoted Burma Shave jingle appears on the cover of a book called *The Verse by the Side of the Road* by Frank Rowserve, Jr. The book captures all 600 of the roadside rhymes.

122   Long after our conversation, *Adweek's Marketing Week* reported that General Motors' Chief Executive Bob Stempel conceded to ABC's Ted Koppel that "no amount of advertising is going to change young consumers' negative perceptions about American cars. That can only be done...by delivering quality...and building word of mouth." (June 17, 1991.)

INDEX